Hawkers Galore

Memories of a Uttoxeter Baker

by

John Walker

Churnet Valley Books

Published by

CHURNET VALLEY BOOKS

43 Bath Street
Leek
Staffordshire
01538 399033

ISBN 1 897949 19 7

Printed in Great Britain by the Ipswich Book Company, Suffolk

Contents

Taken at Rocester in the 1890s. My Grandad is on the left.

With additional drawings by the Author
and Nicola and Sally Richardson

Mr Jesse Jackson, baker, of Denstone (See p.32)

CHAPTER ONE
The Heath Bakery

The Heath Bakery is situated on an area of high ground to the north west of Uttoxeter town centre. This area known as the Heath has an elevated and commanding position over the surrounding district. Although now built up and absorbed into the town itself, a couple of centuries ago it was a quite separate entity of heathland with a few scattered houses and farms. In 1909 the Heath School was built on the farm which belonged to a Mr Miller. Bracken, that most tenacious of plants, is still to be found growing on the little strip of 'no man's land' between the school and the laundry.

The Heath Bakery

The high elevation of this area made it an ideal place to establish a windmill, with its adjacent buildings and connected industries. Two hundred years ago these buildings consisted of the windmill and the miller's house, which was built on to the mill, the bakehouse and old coalhouse, a drying kiln, piggeries and stables. The windmill was offered for sale in the Staffordshire Advertiser of 1809 and described as being 'newly built'. A sale notice acclaimed the mill as 'being on high exposed ground and may be worked without intermission throughout the year.'

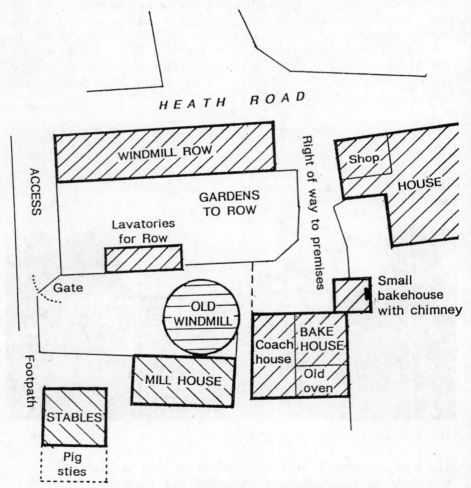

Plan of the buildings as they were in Gregory's time.

Over a hundred years ago, in 1895, when John Gregory died, the whole industry had declined and he was the last miller *and* baker.

This short period of time marked the sudden end of an era where the miller ground his wheat and made bread from it for sale which was more or less typified in the life of John Gregory. The general commercial use of the windmill ended between the 1880s and the early 1900s.

My friend Horace Mitchell who lived in the village of Laugherton in Lincolnshire told me when he was in his nineties, about his father, also Horace Mitchell, who was the miller and baker to the village. Although Horace was never in the trade himself – he became a poultry farmer after surviving the Great War – he told me about how he had to help his father when he was a boy. Quite often strong winds would develop in the middle of the night, and they would both get up and go to the windmill to begin their grinding. Advantage had to be taken of good winds to compensate for periods of very little wind. Horace didn't like this intrusion on his sleep though, and much preferred accompanying his mother on the bread rounds!

The windmill was demolished in two stages. About 1905 the cap and sails were removed and also the top three stories of the mill. The ground floor and first floor were left, roofed over with corrugated sheets with the sails propped up against the side. This building was left for another twenty years before being demolished and its materials used in the construction of a house in Holly Road.

The miller's house was demolished about 1938 and today only the bakehouse and the stables are still in existence. The stables are now used as a storeplace by gardeners on the adjacent allotments.

When John Gregory died he was succeeded by his young apprentice, Joshua Blore, in 1895. Jos was a most exemplary man – he was already a part time soldier in the Uttoxeter Volunteers. He is pictured on the following page at the age of twenty one on Salisbury Plain with the Volunteers in 1900.

Back row, left to right: Not known Not known Tom Hollins
George Stubbs, Jos Blore, Tom Lunn, Jack Prince (chimney sweep)
In front: Dido Price Not known Jim Motteram

The Uttoxeter Volunteers on Salisbury Plain 1900
Jos Blore standing 5th from left back row.

Jos was a very skilled baker and confectioner. He won the first prize, a Gold Medal, for bread at the International Exhibition in London in 1905. The following year he won it again and the Heath Bakery became known as 'The Gold Medal Bakery' for the rest of Jos Blore's time there.

But alas, the World War began in August 1914; Jos

volunteered for the Army at the age of 37 and became a baker in the Army Service Corps. His customers all told him they would come back to him on his return.

When the war finished, human nature being what it is, Jos Blore's customers who had now gone elsewhere, did not return to him. He struggled to regain his former business, but he was only a shadow of his earlier self. He had suffered war wounds and had been gassed and only carried on with extreme difficulty. His wife helped him to mix the bread and his young sons and daughter also gave assistance, but all to no avail – his health gradually deteriorated. My Father bought the Heath Bakery in November 1929 and Jos died the following year at the age of 53.

Jos Blore and his wife Miriam

Windmill and Miller's House – about 1900. The bakehouse is obscured by the windmill and the lavatory building on the foreground.

CHAPTER TWO
The early days

When my parents took over the bakery business, the property was in very poor repair and there was a gaping hole in the blue tiled roof, just above the loft door. There was no stock, only a few pounds of currants, some flour and some sugar. Customers were few and far between then in the 'slump' – the great recession of the thirties.

Mr Hough (pronounced Huff) was a flour traveller for Vernons, a leading firm of flour millers. He supplied my Grandad with flour at Rocester and came to see my Dad with a view to supplying him also. Credit was unheard of in the thirties and if a baker required flour he had to pay for it immediately. Mr Hough knew my father had no money so he kindly allowed him to have a delivery of flour and pay for it after he had made it into bread and sold it. This put my Father on his feet and we have never had our bread flour from any other firm – although Vernons is no longer in existence by that name. It is now part of Spillers.

The bakehouse had no shop, so everything that was made had to be taken and hawked from door to door on bread rounds, as they were known. My Dad had fortunately been used to delivery work when he was a butcher's boy at Denstone. My father was actually a pork butcher 'by trade' although he had knowledge of the bakery business because his father, my grandfather worked as a baker for Andrew Dwyer of Rocester, and my father had also worked there for a few years. Grandad had always said that baking was a life of hard work and long hours, and he did not want to see his sons in the trade. When his eldest son Harry left school, he got a job in the office at Rocester railway station. Likewise, when my Dad left school, his father fixed him up with a job as a porter on the station!

My Dad did not take the job, but instead secured himself employment at Bernard Atkin's, a butcher at Denstone. He 'lived in' and in fact never lived at home again – although (or perhaps as a result) maintaining an excellent relationship with his parents. He soon found out what a hard life he was to have here. At night when he went into the house after killing all day, he would put his wet boots in front of the fire to dry and Bernard Atkin would come in, pick the boots up, take them to the door and kick them down the yard into the road.

In summer they would very often have sheep's head broth for their dinner, sheep's heads having a very limited sale in hot weather. He said when this broth was served out there would be maggots, stretched out and floating on top. You had to skim these off with your spoon! When my Dad went out at night, courting my Mother, he would find the door locked on his return and would have to sleep in the horses' stables. When Bernard discovered what he was doing, he locked up the stables and my Dad had to sleep in the calves' shed. Despite all this, my Dad said that Bernard was an excellent butcher and he soon learnt the trade from him. So not surprisingly, when my parents started at the Heath Bakery, a lot of butchers' products were made, such as sausage, brawn, pork pies and savoury ducks as well as bakery goods.

The extremely hard work and diligence of my parents soon made the bakehouse a 'going concern' and they were able to buy a few machines – one at a time! Before they bought a machine for mincing meat, my mother used a household hand mincer – clamped on the edge of a table. She put three pigs through this machine! On Tuesdays they worked all day and then all night preparing goods for Wednesday which was Market Day.

My Dad had a natural flair for selling and dealing with people and he never took advantage of other people's misfortunes. I well remember a very poor family in Uttoxeter where the father was unemployed and where there were many children. My Dad used to leave them bread and essential groceries and a one pound note on the table every week. This was in the slump of the 30s when my Dad would also be struggling to survive.

His success in business was mainly due to not having any waste. He was opposed to it in any shape or form. There was always a 'pig churn' at the rear of the bakehouse; my Father looked in this quite regularly and woe betide anyone who had used it! I once spoilt a pan of custards (about 60 small custards). I had to dig a hole and bury them – I daren't put them in the pig churn – they were so over baked that I don't think the pigs would have appreciated them anyway!

My Father and Mother —— Jack and Olive Walker

On the subject of waste, my Father would say: "If you waste one loaf a day and perhaps a small cake and a bun, this may not seem much but it adds up to..... seven shillings a day (in the 1970s). This is forty two shillings a week – that is £109 a year – that will licence and insure your van for a year." It is quite easy to crush a loaf or drop a cake or other small product, so you had to pay a great deal of attention to what you were doing.

During the 1930s my parents did a lot of competition work – exhibiting at London, Birmingham and Manchester etc. My Mother, who was an artist, attended evening classes at Stafford, learning the art of cake decoration in icing sugar. Every year she not only won prizes for her work there, but also prizes for the best student in the class. She was soon taking prizes at the national and international competitions. Her greatest achievement was winning the second prize, a silver medal, at the International Bakers' Exhibition in London. She won this in open competition with cake decorators throughout the world. The cake that took first prize came from Johannesburg in South Africa and arrived just a couple of hours before the judging took place!

My Dad also won many prizes for bread; a bronze medal and third prize at London, and many other awards throughout Great Britain. I remember he had a small mangle at the bakehouse which he used to obtain a nice uniform texture in his exhibition doughs. How ever they found the time to do all this extra work I just don't know! But with the advent of the war in 1939, all the exhibitions were finished. The war also brought a dire shortage of bakery materials and a scarcity of labour and these shortages not only lasted for the six years of wartime, but also continued into the early 1950s. And then my Mother's great talents were brought to an end with the onset of Parkinson's Disease in the mid forties.

I think that the diligence, competence and sheer hard work of my parents was best summed up by my neighbour at the bakehouse, many years later. It was a summer night and I had just finished work for the day; it was 9.45pm. My neighbour Jack Elliot was in his garden and he came to the side window of the bakehouse and said: "John, you put some time in here, you do. But you'll never do the work that your father and mother have done here – not as long as ever you live."

CHAPTER THREE
On the bread round

Quite often, as a boy, I would accompany my father on his bread rounds, sitting on a small folding seat, fixed in the van cab. At some of his calls he would stay for some time, having a cup of tea. If these customers happened to spot me in the van, they would call me to come in also. On these journeys I would be very observant of nature and I quite enjoyed these long 'outings'.

In summertime I would take a carrier bag and while my Dad was making calls I would gradually fill it with dandelions, nettles and eriff for making herb beer. I made this myself – my Mother supervising the boiling! The herbs were tipped out into a jam kettle and as much water put to them to enable the whole to simmer for twenty minutes without boiling over. The herbs were then strained through a colander into an enamel bucket, and the liquor, which was very dark and strong, was made up to about ¾ of a bucket with cold water. A two pound bag of sugar was stirred in and a piece of toast spread with yeast floated on top. This was left until next day when the toast was removed and the liquor bottled. After a day or two it was ready for drinking!

I would get quite hungry on these delivery rounds. On the Denstone round I could not wait to get to the Tavern – here my Dad would go in and have a glass of beer and a small pie. He would say to me: "You can come and have a cake." I would get out and go to the back of the van, where he would pull trays of cakes out and say to me, "Take one." I was allowed just one cake and I always chose a milk cake. This was like a plain scone but bigger than the fruit scones or any of the other cakes – and more filling! He often would tell me, "My Dad always let me have a cake when I was a boy."

I would go back to the cab and relish every crumb of that milk cake! Sometimes when we were driving along empty country lanes, my Dad would slow down and I was allowed to steer the van!

One of my earliest jobs in the bakehouse was to dissolve the yeast in a bowl of warm water. I didn't at first like putting my hand into this gluey mass and my Dad would say, "Come on, get that yeast dissolved – it won't bite you!" As a boy of 10 or

11 years and older, I was conscripted into delivering bread for my Father. He fixed me up with a red notebook and pencil; the notebook had a list of customers in it, all within a reasonable walking distance of the bakehouse. I would fill my basket with bread and set off, returning again to refill it as necessary. This was always my Saturday morning job and my Dad gave me my pocket money on a Saturday. I had a halfpenny a week for some years, then he increased it to a penny, but then some weeks he forgot to give it to me at all!

I found some of the customers on my list to be hard, unyielding people – they didn't give a damn for bakers' boys or anyone else! There was Mrs Mottram in the small pebble-dashed cottage on Cheadle Road. She wore a huge shawl and had her ginger hair in long plaits down her back and she fixed you with her deep brown eyes the moment you entered her living room – like a stoat transfixes a rabbit before the kill. Mrs Mottram would tell me how many loaves she wanted and then would fire at me, "How much do I owe you, John?" I would get my pencil and red notebook into operation, not being very good at arithmetic, and then I would deliver the result. "Oh no, I don't," would be the reply as she reached to the mantlepiece for pen and paper. Then, in large black figures, she would do the offending sum correctly, saying: "That's what I owe you and I shan't rob you or pay you any more than I need to!"

Mrs Wheeler was the wife of the Uttoxeter Postmaster and lived in Holly Road. My Dad always said: "Make sure everyone pays – or they don't have any more bread." But I didn't know Mrs Wheeler paid every so often by cheque. One Saturday I left a note under her door with the amount owing. Mrs Wheeler asked my Father what was going on, and said she would get her bread elsewhere. I ended up getting a roasting for that. I seemed to have some real sticklers to deal with.

In 1948 when I was older and started work for my father, I very soon realised what grand people all my customers were, after all. Mrs Mottram, to whom I have just referred, was always most kind, friendly and hospitable. Even then it was some years before I realised how and why my Dad had compiled that particular list of customers for me when I was at school. They were all good, straightforward people, who stood no 'messing about' – thus upholding one of my Dad's favourite axioms: "The people who stand up to you are in the end the only people who will stand by you."

MILK CAKES

CHAPTER FOUR
The post-war years

I came into the bakery business in 1948 when I was 'demobbed' from the Army. My service in the Army gave me plenty of time to think about my choice of career in 'Civvy Street' as we called it. More or less, I had three choices; Barclays Bank, which had been my last job, and which was preferred by my mother – mainly because of the short hours of work, the holidays and the pension provided. I did not care much for this indoor work, and to me, what were the bank's tedious tasks.

Then there was the life of farming, also available to me as my Dad had a smallholding at Winnoth Dale. This was more attractive as I liked farming, having done farm work at Parkside, Abbots Bromley. Also this more reclusive life appealed to my introverted nature; I did not particularly enjoy meeting people, and I was so readily embarrassed in other people's company – for no reason!

Then there was the third choice of the bakery trade with its hard work, exceptionally long hours and lack of time off. And again, I would have to be meeting people all the time, hawking bread from door to door and standing at the market stall. In other words, my living would depend on my ability to make *and to sell* that which I produced.

But I eventually made my decision to go into the bakery trade while I was stationed at Mount Carmel near Haifa in Palestine, and I wrote and told my parents. They never tried to influence me in any way. My Dad, of course, told me of the hard work involved, but to me this was a challenge and one I readily accepted. He said: "Don't think there is a lot of money to be made in baking – there isn't. What money I have made, I have made from dealing." My Dad would buy and sell anything; motor cars, furniture, property – anything!

It was the first week in May when the troopship brought our Regiment, the K.S.L.I., back from Port Said in Egypt to Liverpool. Everywhere in England was clothed in the beautiful fresh green colours of spring – what a contrast to the arid landscape of the North African desert. After a few more weeks I was 'demobbed' and returned home. My Dad said: "Well, John, when are you starting work?" I was surprised and said: "I was going to have a week or two holiday." "Holiday?" my Dad said. "You don't want any holiday. If you start having holidays, you will never want to do any work as long as you live." I started work next day!

On my first day at the bakehouse he said: "You can come round with me in the van and I will show you where we call with bread. You will soon get used to it all." Every house on our delivery rounds was called on either two or three times each week. The delivery rounds covered five districts and were as follows:

Monday morning	Denstone and Stubwood
Monday afternoon	Stramshall
Tuesday	Uttoxeter and Bramshall
Wednesday	Uttoxeter Market Days Stall
	– no rounds
Thursday morning	Uttoxeter and Denstone
Thursday afternoon	Stramshall
Friday morning	Rocester and Stubwood
Friday afternoon	Bramshall
Saturday	Uttoxeter and Stramshall

Away we went on these rounds, me calling at some houses, my Dad at others, but he only took me on a round once! After that I was on my own! I soon knew which houses and farms to call on, but the council house estates in the villages were quite a problem – all the houses looked the same! For a time or two I would go up to doors and knock and then have to say: "Does my Dad call here?"

In these days of wrapping and bagging all foodstuffs, sometimes several layers of wrappings, it is strange to recall the days when very few bakery goods were wrapped. Bread was never wrapped at all, from the time it left the oven until it was eaten! This also applied to currant bread and all goods of a 'solid nature' such as fruit cakes, madeira cake, slab cake and pork pies. Only fancy cakes, such as cream filled goods, were put into paper bags at the point of sale. Even then this was not done for any hygenic reason, but to prevent them from being damaged and also to prevent them from smearing other goods with cream or sugar. When selling from the delivery basket or from the van, people would fetch a plate from the house for their cakes.

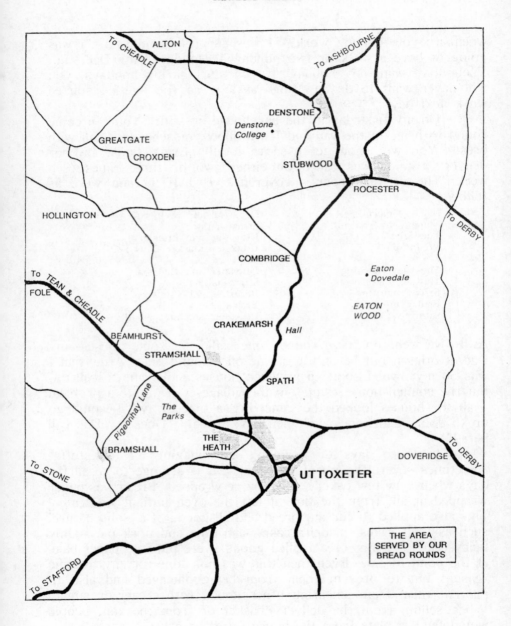

THE AREA
SERVED BY OUR
BREAD ROUNDS

CHAPTER FIVE
The bakehouse

Before I go any further, perhaps it would be as well for me to describe the bakehouse as it was when I arrived in 1948. Apart from the necessary repairs which my father had carried out – mending the roof, putting a new floor in the flour loft and putting in stairs – the place was more or less the same as when Jos Blore left it in 1930.

Jos's old blue truck was still in the storeroom shown on this plan. The storeroom had at one time been a bakehouse in its own right, complete with oven and chimney. Old Dick Hodgkinson, who lived nearby, said that the two bakehouses were once kept by two brothers, and that neither of them spoke to each other. He didn't remember them, but was quite adamant about the truth of this story.

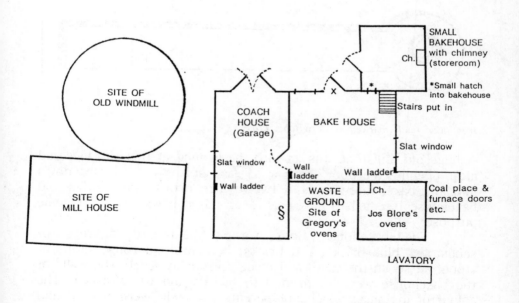

Plan of Bakehouse in 1948

The bakehouse is by far the oldest part, all the other rooms being later additions. The whole was roofed in blue tiles; the bakehouse was built of a narrow, hard red brick, the coachhouse was built on in a larger pale, poor quality brick. Pieces of bond wood are used in the bakehouse building, pieces of oak of varying length put in the brickwork here and there (? to save bricks).

The door into the bakehouse (marked 'X' on the plan) was an old plank door which must have been there for a century at least. It had a big finger hole in it to lift a large latch on the outside of the door. This latch had the mark of a witch's cross on it; the loft door, which had a smaller latch, also had one of these crosses. In fact, on my travels, I came across many of these iron latches. The diagonal cross was supposed to keep away evil spirits from the premises! The cross was always contained by a vertical line on each side, as illustrated below.

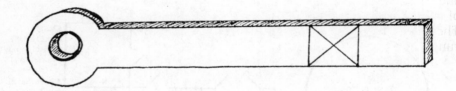

Iron door latch marked with witch's cross

A huge old millstone was let into the ground at this entrance and after opening the door there was – and still is – a big step down into the bakehouse (about a twelve inch drop). Some other old bakehouses seemed to have this 'drop', as if it was done for some purpose.

The bakehouse floor was a haphazard mixture of sandstone, blue bricks, red bricks, boulders and rough limps of stone, all set in the earth and made reasonably level. The walls of the bakehouse were all lined with boards and whitewashed. The colourful diplomas which my parents had won were framed and hanging on the walls; also several 'Factory Acts' which had to be prominently displayed by law.

The ceiling was underdrawn in the same boards, and these were as black as ink; blackened with smoke from the ovens and furnaces. Long peels were used for putting the baking in and out of the oven. These were kept resting on a couple of spars, tacked on to the low beam. Coal had to be carried through the bakehouse and tipped up into the small stoke hole. The big cast iron 'front' of the ovens had on it 'Bentley – Stoke on Trent 1903'. Before these ovens were installed by Jos Blore, I am quite certain that Gregory's ovens would have been on the area of 'waste ground' and opening into the bakehouse. In fact the wall marked § was a very thick convex wall in the coach house and built of the small hard, narrow bricks.

Wall ladders were in the positions shown and went through a small square opening onto the flour loft above the bakehouse. It was not possible to carry a sack of flour through these openings! Before my father had the stairs built, a hoist was used. This hoist projected from the bakehouse roof over the door and the loft door which was just under the hoist. This same type of wall ladder is still to be found in the stable buildings nearby. They are difficult to use as there is only a 'toe hold' on the rungs.

The two windows shown on the plan did not open – or indeed did not need to – as the right hand half of the window was glass and the other side was a 'lattice' or 'slats'. These vertical slats of wood had a half inch gap between them. There was also a row of slats behind them opposite the gaps of the inside row. Perhaps best shown on this plan!

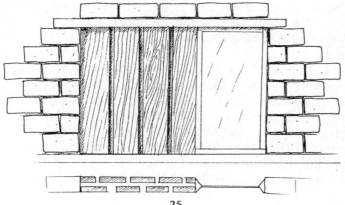

These lattice windows were also in the stables and were to be seen at butchers' shops and most other places where food was prepared.

The storeroom was so called by Jos Blore because he had racks in it, and bread was passed through the small hatch marked on the plan and left in here to cool. We kept boot-polish and brushes and a mirror in this hatch!

The only other room was known as the garage, as we kept the van there overnight. This long room was of whitewashed brick walls and a blue brick floor – a better floor than in the bakehouse itself! The ceiling was not underdrawn and showed the rafters carrying the loft floor above. There were two iron cratches still up on the wall corners, from the time when horses had obviously been kept in here. There was a wall ladder in here too, by the window. This went into the loft above, which could also be entered by a hatch door from the flour loft. This loft over the garage we called the far loft and was mainly used for keeping steps and ladders, spare timber and other useful stuff, most of which was never needed!

We had cold water on tap but not hot water. A gas boiler or 'copper' as we called it was used for all the hot water we needed. Our last job of the day would be the washing up and mopping all the floors – both of them! The copper would then be filled and lit ready for 'mixing'. We mixed the bread dough at about nine o'clock every night. After mixing for about twenty minutes, the machine bowl was tipped and the dough was cut out in pieces, as much as could be carried, and put into the wooden trough (pronounced as in 'low'), the trough having been greased previously. The loose lid was put on and the dough left to rise all night. We usually finished at about quarter to ten, that is my Dad and myself.

In the morning we would arrive for work at about 5.25am. Then Don would arrive. Rhoda came about 8.00am. My first job would be to light the fire in the furnace to get the ovens going. I would use paper and sticks and three shovels of coal; although there were two ovens and furnaces, we only ever used the bottom oven – the top deck was never used. The next job was to 'knock back' the dough. It would have risen well during the night and lifted the lid on top of it. The lid was removed and the dough

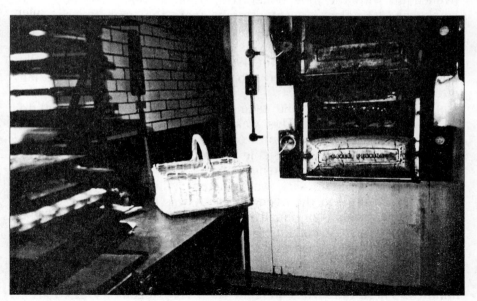

The wooden trough and a basket for delivering bread.

punched down well and folded up to get it as near to its original size as possible. When this knocking back was being done you had to keep turning your head away; the gases from it were so strong, they would take your breath and cause choking. Other jobs followed in an established order – lighting the prover, lighting the copper and so on.

After about half an hour, the dough would have risen very much and would be cut out of the trough and thrown on to the lightly floured table. It was weighed off into pieces, each of 2lb, and these were either moulded into shape by hand or put through a moulding machine, which we now had, saving a lot of work. The moulded pieces of dough were dropped into warmed bread tins and placed on racks in the prover, with its warm and steamy atmosphere, created by boiling a bowl of water on a gas ring.

While these jobs were going on, the oven fire would have to be constantly tended. After the fire was going well, it was levelled out along the firebars and a further three shovels of coal thrown along it. This produced a very hot, bright fire which was livened up with the long poker from time to time. The heat, the smoke and the flames went straight from the open furnace into the oven which it heated, and out through the chimney shown on the plan. A further three shovels of coal would be used to get the oven up to 'bread heat', about 490°F. The bread in its tins in the prover would be ready after about another 45 minutes for going into the oven.

Before baking could take place, another operation had to be carried out though. This was 'mopping out'. When the oven door was opened, the interior would be full of soot, hanging from the oven crown and on the sole of the oven. A mop with a very long stale and a sack fastened on its end, was dipped into a bucket of water. The sack was twisted round in the bucket and quickly lifted up into the oven, where it was unwound and swirled around and around, continually dipping it into the bucket until the oven was cleaned of hanging soot and other matter.

Then the damper was pushed in to retain the heat and the bread was set in the oven, two loaves being loaded with the peel at a time and carefully set in the oven to bake for about fifty minutes. These old ovens were lit by a very ingenious 'gas flare'. It consisted of about four iron gas pipes, each about twenty inches long and joined together by brass 'hinges'. These allowed the gas to pass along them. When the pipes were folded together one on top of another on the oven front, the 'hinges' cut off nearly all the gas supply and left just enough to allow a small pilot light to burn at the end. When the fitting was swung around and pushed into the oven, extending the pipes, the 'hinges' would allow the full volume of gas through and the oven interior was lit by the fierce yellow flame over two feet in length. I loved 'having a go' with this when I was a boy.

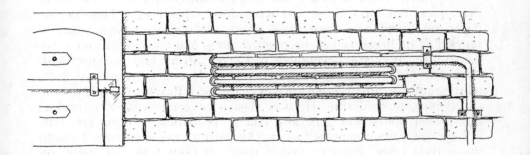

The Gas Flare

Whilst the bread was baking we had our breakfast. Of course many other jobs were done in the morning as well as bread making; short paste was made, scones, pork pies, etc. But the Heath Bakery was always mainly a 'bread' bakery; some bakehouses produced more cake than bread – these tended to be bakehouses with shops attached (although during my time at the bakery I introduced a lot more cake and other confectionery).

When the bread was baked, one person would draw it out of the oven and another would take it out of the tins. The bread was put on the trough or table to cool as much as possible before being packed on the van for delivery. There was very little space for the four of us to work in this small room but we seemed to manage all right!

CHAPTER SIX
Transport

Bread would be delivered by Don and myself and we would leave the bakehouse as soon after nine o'clock as possible. For instance, on Mondays I would set out and deliver bread to Denstone and Stubwood, returning about two o'clock. Then Don would reload the van and do the Stramshall round, finishing about five o'clock. When we were not delivering, of course, we were working in the bakehouse.

In the early days a truck was pushed around for local town deliveries, but later these too were done with a van. This locally delivered bread was done by a youth with a large basket and a truck full of bread which he pushed along the road. Like our own bakehouse, Parker's bakehouse in Carter Street had no shop and they had an old basket-work truck with one of the two side wheels cutting into the wickerwork! Herbert Fearn or 'Pip', as we called him, pushed this. He was always covered in flour from his cap to his boots and generally had a 'Woodbine' on the go! The Co-op had rather narrow red trucks with a cambered top. I think these had a few runners inside them to hold trays of buns or cakes as well as the bread.

Our truck was a heavy wooden one, painted blue and with an iron rail around the lid to prevent the basket sliding off. It held about forty 2lb loaves. It was always a problem to pack the warm bread so that it would not crush. An even bigger problem was the steam which condensed on the cold sides of vans and trucks and ran down like a river, soaking the bread and completely spoiling it. We used to line the truck and van with empty flour bags; thick, heavy hessian bags, returnable to the millers with money charged on each one.

After this truck, which had been Jos Blore's before us, we had 'Ivy', best described as a truck propelled by the rear half of a bicycle. The name 'IVY' was painted on the frame. This was a really smart turnout and I have never seen one like it – either before or since! It had an opening lid and also a door in the front which was opened with a carriage key. She would hold about thirty five 1lb loaves, although in use we would carry less, as we also had to have small loaves and Hovis. Ivy could move along quite fast on a level road but like the lady she was, she had a hidden vice! To make a left or right hand turn had to be done very slowly indeed or otherwise Ivy would immediately jack-knife and the weighty truck part would turn at right angles and go down onto the road. The rider would be thrown off at once joining Ivy on the road. Even then the game was not over, Ivy had developed it into a fine art; the truck lid would fly open – even the front door would be sprained open – and all the bread would disgorge onto the road! And she even had her favourite spots for this performance where there was always likely to be a good supply of onlookers!

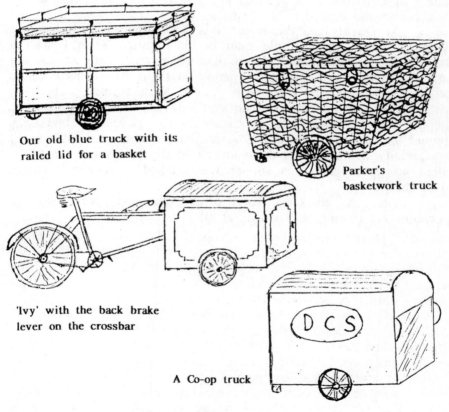

Our old blue truck with its railed lid for a basket

Parker's basketwork truck

'Ivy' with the back brake lever on the crossbar

A Co-op truck

Some bread trucks used in Uttoxeter

Even the smallest villages had their own bakehouse and baker; I remember Mr Fradley, the last baker at Bramshall. At Rocester there were three bakehouses – my Grandad worked in one of them for Andrew Dwyer and later for his son Tom Dwyer. The baker at Denstone was Jesse Jackson, an old man who had fought in the Boer War in South Africa in 1899. His father was a baker at Denstone before him.

Jesse finished baking about 1949. One day he had all his doughs mixed and his bread in tins ready for baking when he was taken ill and died. Obviously, with all the unattended doughs, everything was soon a terrible mess. Arthur Carter, who was a baker at Denstone College, dug a big hole in the field behind the bakehouse and buried it all – tins as well!

At Doveridge, the baker was Teddy Bates with his son George. Teddy was an old man in his eighties when I started baking in the late forties. Even then he started work at 4.00am and did more work than many people in their twenties! He was a small, hawk–eyed old man with a Lord Roberts moustache. His early life had been hard and he said little about it normally, but he did tell me once that, as a boy in the 1870s, he had been bound apprentice to Bakewells at Sudbury. When the day's work was finally over, he would be locked in the bakehouse where he slept on flour bags. His supper was pushed in to him through iron bars!

Yes, we all knew each other well and there was no acrimonious rivalry between us at all.

CHAPTER SEVEN
Tramps and hawkers

Ours were all good 'close-knit' rounds, calling on nearly every house and farm in the area. Some farms would have thirty six loaves a week, twelve on each of their three calls. I knew all of the people so well; they were soon not only customers but friends. I knew their parents and grandparents, their children and grandchildren, even some of their birthdays!

Likewise I shared in their joys and their sorrows. My Dad insisted on a golden rule: "Nothing must be repeated from one house to another." During the course of many years hawking from house to house, one soon met and knew the other regular callers, such as milkmen, postmen, butchers' boys, window cleaners and other bread delivery men. We also became acquainted with the less regular hawkers such as peddlers, gypsies and tramps on their travels around the countryside. About once a year I would meet old Mrs Gypsy Finney, dressed completely in black, accompanied by her more colourful daughters. They sold meat tins, kettles, pans, lace, clothes pegs and other small items.

Jack Bannister and his 'wife' were two tramps – she always walked about twenty yards behind him. Every so often they would stop and have a slanging match, raising their fists up to each other, sometimes actually fighting, before trudging on. I never knew whether this was done to arouse pity and elicit food and gifts or if it was real warfare! They slept the night in barns. Wintertime was spent in Mellor's barn at New Road, Uttoxeter.

When tramps were questioned about their trade or working ability they would often refer to themselves as 'milestone inspectors'. They had an excellent method of making tea, after the manner of gypsies and other 'roadsters'. A tea can containing water is hung over a fire (rain

Tea can with 'cup' lid. 1½ or 2 pints

33

water makes the best tea). As soon as the water boils the can is removed and a spoonful of tea is sprinkled onto it, followed by a spoonful of sugar, if used. Next the milk if required, is stirred in. This makes a grand cup of tea.

Every Friday the oatcake man came to Rocester, on the train from Macclesfield, with a couple of big wicker baskets full of oatcakes. These were left at the station while he hawked them from door to door with a smaller basket.

Another character, 'America Jack' pushed a pram full of buckets, brushes and 'lime', and flying from the front of the pram was the Union Jack. He had been deported to Northern Canada in the late 1800s for poaching rabbits, then when the Great War broke out, convicts were given a free pardon if they were willing to serve in the armed forces. Jack served with the Canadian army in France; he served with distinction and at the end of the war returned to England a free man. He then began his life of whitewashing farmers' barns with his pram-borne equipment! His real name was John Salt and he came from Prestwood near Ellastone. Opposite is a picture taken of him in Oak Lane, Denstone, sitting on the roadside bank opposite to Bernard Atkin's butcher's shop and enjoying a snack Mrs Atkin has given him. Look at the whitewash on his socks and boots!

Joby Bloor from Uttoxeter went round with a pony and flat dray selling blocks of salt around farms, with his red and white spotted 'muffler' round his neck and a flat crowned boater style hat. There were always one or two lurchers following under the back of the dray, ready to chase – and catch – a rabbit or two!

Cups, saucers, plates and all manner of pottery was taken from door to door and these were generally carried in a large clothes basket by two people working together.

The knife grinder also came round on his bike. When a householder wanted shears, scissors or knives sharpening, the grinder would turn his bike upside down and the pedals would then operate the small grinding wheel attachment to great effect!

'Paraffin Harry' delivered his goods every fortnight coming round in a large van. As his name implies, he sold paraffin and also brushes, kettles, tins, fire irons and other hardware and utensils. A lot of paraffin was used for cooking

America Jack

stoves. These small 'tin' stoves had an oven and one, or more usually, two rings for a saucepan or kettle.

Another traveller, often an Indian, would lug a huge bulging suitcase from door to door, full of every item of clothing one could imagine. He would knock on the door and immediately open the case on the ground, deftly exposing and arranging all its contents in the case and the lid – ready for the opening door!

Other 'packmen', as we called them, would have a shallow wooden box about two feet square with a hinged lid. This flat case was carried by a leather strap slung aroung the neck. At the door they would slide the box round in front of them and open the lid. The lid and bottom were then like two big trays, filled with every conceivable item a housewife might want. There was a grand array of buttons, needles, thread, laces, buckles, combs, brooches and so on; a veritable Aladdin's cave.

Mr Surtees lived near the bakehouse. He would cycle round farms and houses taking orders for his cattle and horse oils and ointments, and also for boot and shoe polish. This polish was in proper tins with his own printed labels – it was called 'Bootine'. When he had gathered his orders, he would spend other days cycling out to deliver the goods.

My Dad used to say: "Going round in the pouring rain, knocking on doors for 'no thank you – not today'; if this won't break your heart then nothing will!"

CHAPTER EIGHT
The bakehouse – enlargements and alterations

From 1950, over a few years, we altered the bakehouse completely. My father bought some land from the local council – the hatched area on the plan – where the Mill House had been. A new building was erected here to house a double decked Baker Perkins oven. This oven had been little used where it had been installed at the High Street property of Messrs Elkes. It was rebuilt and installed for us by its makers, Baker Perkins of Peterborough. It was a "steam tube" oven, heated by coke. About a hundred thick tubes went over the top and underneath each oven, the ends of the tubes being in the furnace. Each tube was very thick and hollow, containing a small amount of oil. When the heat boils this liquid, the vapour being unable to escape, develops a great heat. These were so much cleaner than the old coal ovens which we had removed some years later; no 'mopping out', a more even temperature in the oven, a level steel sole instead of the uneven square firebricks – so much better all round.

We had our coke delivered from Uttoxeter Gas Works, good coke in large lumps about as big as a dinner plate, which we hit with the back of the shovel to make it into egg size pieces. Only a few years later the Gas Works finished and we had coke brought in from Birmingham. This coke was of a much poorer quality and very dusty, as it was loaded with a mechanical loading shovel, whereas the Uttoxeter coke was loaded with a fork!

Then industrial strikes started to occur and we had difficulty in getting the coke; so after a few years of this we had the ovens converted to oil. Most of the conversion was done over a long weekend and resulted in a huge pile of debris outside the bakehouse. My son David who was in the Royal Artillery, came over on leave and using the contractor's small lorry, he removed all this debris to the tip. Most difficult to handle, the debris consisted of sand and bricks, stone and assorted iron work and of course no shortage of soot! All the oven conversion was done by Tills of Bristol, bakery engineers, and was another big improvement for us.

The coachhouse was built up, half way across it, and the open ground, where Gregorys' ovens had been, covered in and

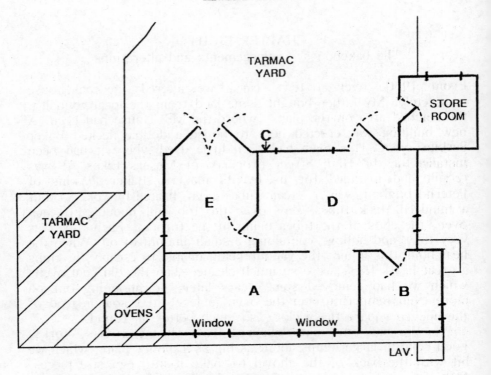

Alterations and enlargements in the 1950s

rebuilt to provide another room – 'A' on the plan. The whole place was lined with white glazed bricks for the upper half and red bricks for the lower. The roof timbers had deteriorated and were replaced and the whole was roofed in asbestos corrugated sheets. The exterior walls were all rendered and finished in a weatherproof paint. The yard was re-tarmaced in about 1960 and Jos Blore's ovens at last removed to provide another room – 'B' on the plan. This room we use mainly for storage.

There had been a single door (C) into the bakehouse at some early date, the brickwork of it being quite noticeable before the stucco work was done. When the tarmac work was done we had an access path made along the rear of the premises to the old lavatory in order to keep the place in good order. This old lavatory had a wooden seat and also a smaller seat for a child! But this was not as old as the rest of the property – a different brick yet again.

Some years ago I was talking to old Jim Myatt, a first world war veteran. Jim could not read or write but he had an exceptional memory for people, places and names. He was brought up by his grandparents at Heath Cross and he said that his grandad remembered the windmill working. His grandad said that one day a man called to see the miller and tethered his donkey to one of the sails. When the fellow came out, a gust of wind had taken the donkey up into the air! I doubted the truth of this but old Jim was insistent: "My grandad would never tell a lie!"

Of course the sails on a tower mill such as this come quite close to the ground and do indeed cause a hazard, and I realised that old Jim's story could have been true.

Picture of our van, Big Emma, taken by the gate to Denstone Vicarage

CHAPTER NINE
On the road and in the market

In the forties and fifties, delivering bread by motor van had many problems. These vehicles, their engines, their batteries, etc, were nowhere near as reliable as today's vehicles. Punctures were also more prevalent as well as other mechanical faults. And again, winter conditions were more extreme, but in this mainly low lying area, floods were the constant problem – they of course occurred in summer as well as in winter! This trouble has to a great extent disappeared today with the mechanised digging out and clearing of ditches, brooks and rivers. During floods, I have walked along the top of a wall to deliver bread to Ede's farm at Waterloo. It was also very tricky at Stramshall Mill, as the water was not only deep but also had a strong current which at times would move the van about and be quite scary!

Country people would ask me to take their accumulators or 'wet batteries' to the garage to be recharged for their wireless sets. This was always accompanied by the stern admonition: "Now don't you go and tip it over or spill it!"

An old wireless accumulator of the 30s

The picture opposite is of the first van that I had, a 1927 Austin. It was originally a car belonging to a wealthy local farmer, Mr Albert Abnett of Grindley. During the war he lent it for service as an ambulance at Coventry. We had this coach-built body put on it, made by Hovis at Macclesfield and lettered in gold leaf. We nicknamed her 'Big Emma'!

The trust which people had in one another was something to be admired. I would meet people walking into town from outlying areas and they would say, for example, "The door's open, John. My purse is on the mantlepiece; if there's not enough change, there's a ten shilling note under the candlestick." At times I have given change in a house and left my wallet on a piece of furniture – it would not be long before the customer spotted it and came running up the road with it.

Many would let me decide how much bread they would need until my next call, saying: "Have a look in the dairy, John, and see what bread I've got left, then leave what you think!"

People who like myself, went from door to door, also had an unwritten responsibility for the welfare of these, our customers. To give you an insight into this, I remember calling on Miss Avery, who lived in a small cottage across a field at Stubwood – I called every Monday and Friday. One particular Friday I went across and she said: "Do you know, Mr.Walker, you're the first person I've seen since you were here on Monday?" I remember that she always said that "two hours sleep before midnight is worth any amount after". She would sometimes give me a small medicine bottle full of whiskey to give to her brother Alf at Stramshall. He had Parkinson's disease. She would say: "Don't you let his wife know about it!" Imagine the difficulty I had doing that!

Every Wednesday was Market Day in Uttoxeter, a very busy day; but it made an excellent break from the week's delivery rounds. For a few years I stood with my Dad, before he eventually gave it up. For most of the thirty years I was there, I would arrive about 7.30am and unload my van – this would take about half an hour – and then take the van to the park and return to the stall for business. The first job was to fetch a pot of tea from the Milk Bar! This was shared with Gint Sargeant, the butcher, who paid for it every other week. After this I didn't have any more to eat or drink until after market – my Dad never tolerated eating or drinking in front of customers.

The bread and cakes were set out in the same order each week; people then knew where everything was. Cakes of a similar appearance in colour, such as scones, eccles cakes and Nelson cake were never put next to each other; a row of such as iced cakes or butterfly cakes would be put between them to give a good colour break and to show each other up better. Pork pies and sausage rolls were never placed near sugared goods, for instance doughnuts. One had to have enough cakes to make a good show, but at the same time nothing had to be piled too high, this tending to give an impression that the cakes were being treated with contempt instead of care! Each customer was welcomed individually and by name and, after the transaction, was bid good day in a similar fashion. Yeast has always been sold on the stall, providing a service to those who make their own bread, buns, wine or beer.

Trade at the stall was naturally always very subject to the weather. I noticed that on nice sunny and hot days people tended to buy less than on colder or even wet days. It was always a real problem keeping the goods safe from the effects of rain and snow. One particular Wednesday there were only four stalls. There had been overnight snow and it was still snowing in the market and the stalls were put together in a square to combat the swirling snow. When our goods have been made, they have to be sold – unlike clothing and most other market items.

Wasps were another major nuisance from the end of July until the middle of September. Rain never made much difference to them, but a drop in temperature was more effective. Nothing could be done about them. As I would say to my customers, "They are cleaner than flies; a wasp doesn't go on anything dirty."

Although I stood there in the market for so long, I have never walked round the stalls in the market! When I first went to the stall in the late forties, the beautiful silver coinage of Queen Victoria was still in common use, as were the silver 3d pieces. We called them 'threp'ny bits'; other people called them 'Joeys'. But can you imagine my amazement at first when some of the old ladies who came to the stall lifted up their clothes when they came to pay me? These old people always kept their purse in their knickers!! I soon got used to it all!

The busiest time at the stall has always been from 10.00am until midday. I would be more or less sold out by 2.30pm and ready for dinner! A scheme was devised at the end of the 1960s to do away with the market as we know it. Consultants had been approached and a plan made which provided for a permanent market site on the Maltings. A meeting between council officials and stall holders was held in the Town Hall. A large proportion of the ninety nine stall holders attended this meeting, which was held on a Wednesday evening. Many of these people still had to return home, which for some meant several hours travelling time.

The plan was unfolded to us: rows and rows of nice, tidy,

metal framed stalls each with a blue and white roof sheet. These stalls were to be permanently fixed on the precinct car park. The awful traffic congestion would be alleviated in the town. Anyone selling foodstuffs, such as ourselves and butchers, etc, were to be housed together in the Town Hall. We were told this would be much more hygienic and far more comfortable than standing outside in all weathers!

The officials had overlooked one important fact – and hoped we would do the same: This move would have been the death of another of Great Britain's ancient street markets, the market having been held here in the streets for six centuries. After a lot of discussion we rejected the plans completely. For my part, I pointed out that I preferred to buy food outside in the open air – rather than in the confines of a Market Hall, where the enclosed atmosphere was always musty, and crowds of people were coughing and sneezing in the enclosed space. Well, we won the day – I hope for all time – and the officials had to make a dejected exit with all their grand plans!

For some years I stood on the road itself until other stall holders persuaded me to get a board to stand on. I thought I would try it and I found it to be a great help. That piece of old board between the road and one's feet really made a great difference; I felt a lot warmer. Some days in winter the yeast would freeze so solid that it was impossible to break an ounce or two from it and I had to get a knife and chisel a piece off! In these frosts, the cream would be frozen rock hard in the cakes and the pies and sausage rolls were like pieces of wood!

Many of my customers were people that had been to my father and grandfather before me here in the market. This picture of Uttoxeter market shows my Dad at his stall in the thirties. He is standing, hands on

An extract from the postcard showing my father

44

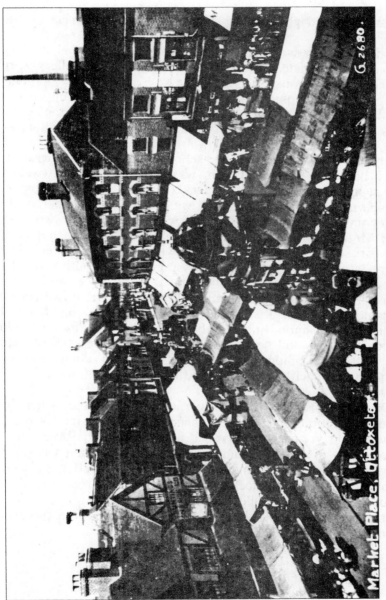

A postcard of Uttoxeter market in the 1930s

45

hips, just to the right of the Dr Johnson's memorial in the centre.

The market was quite a noisy place, as most stall holders bellowed out their trade calls. The fruit and vegetable sellers were particularly vociferous. "Apples a penny a pound, pears......apples..... tomatoes.....plums and pears......tuppence a pound plums", these were some of their calls! In the early seventies the local council sent a letter to all stall holders notifying us that all this shouting would have to cease!

My life long friend and my school teacher, WG Torrance, who, as a boy, lived on the Heath, was a historian of Uttoxeter. One day at my stall in Uttoxeter market he told me the following story which is now history in itself: Mr Torrance remembered old John Gregory well and said that the windmill was not working when he, Mr Torrance, was a boy in the 1890s and had not been working for some years, as the sails were by then rotten. The sails were stopped in the shape of a cross and although the upright sails had slats on them, the sails at right angles were only bare poles. He said that old Gregory had a son in the Royal Navy, whose name was John Risden Gregory. In 1897, the year of Queen Victoria's diamond jubilee, the sailor was at home on leave for the celebrations, and he climbed to the top of the vertical sails and tied there the Union Jack. He said: "I don't know how he dared to go up such a height, as those old slats were really rotten!"

On another occasion, Mr Torrance told me that when he was a boy his mother had made all her own bread. It was made once a week and young Mr Torrance would wheel the bread on a hand cart down to the bakehouse to be baked by John Gregory. The unbaked bread was all marked on top with a letter T, done with a properly made tin dock. Other people also took bread to be baked and it was all collected later in the day. Mr Torrance said that as a boy he was always on the look out for a piece of loose crust – or a piece that could be made loose!

CHAPTER TEN
Some of our customers

I have called at hundreds of houses and farms with my bread, and each and every one has left its own imprint on my memory; perhaps a quaint expression or anecdote, an amusing occurrence or someone's life of dedication; but above all, the kindness and generosity of all these grand people. Most people who write in a similar vein to myself, refer to others by fictitious names, but I have used the peoples' actual names – as there is nothing but good wholesome life to record about these dear folks.

The Bedford van, successor to 'Big Emma'

My Mother used to say to me: "All the people you meet in life are a mirror of your own self." This paradox she explained by saying that if you treat people badly, then they will treat you badly. If you are kind and thoughtful towards others, then they will be the same to you. Likewise if you resent and dislike others, they will resent and dislike you. It didn't take me long to learn the truth of this and also to heed my Father's often respected statement: "Always treat everyone as honest – until you yourself find them otherwise."

Old Tom Jackson was a retired roadman, or 'lengthsman', and lived at Denstone. Before mechanisation, every three or four miles of road had a roadman who used to keep the ditches cleaned out, the grass verges trimmed and the gutters swept clean. These men kept the roads and lanes looking very nice, and each was proud of his own length of road. Tom was a native of the village of Stanton. He was about the last person I knew who spoke in the beautiful language of old England. He pronounced double 'd' as 'th' wherever it occurred. Thus, for example, he would call a 'ladder' a 'lather'. This now only survives in the word 'fodder' – some farmers still talk of 'fother' and 'fothering' their animals. Bedrooms and bedroom windows – Tom would always say 'chambers' and 'chamber windows'; best clothes were 'raiments' and working clothes were 'clouts'!

Tom Jackson, MM

As a youth Tom went into farm service at Stanton. He said they were 'clemmed to death'; being young men the farm workers were always hungry. To help them keep going, he said they would crack an egg on their teeth and down its contents! Also when chance arose they would blow aside the froth on a bucket of milk and have a good draught of that. They rarely had flesh meat (as he called it) for dinner, it was usually boiled fat bacon, nothing but fat. Sometimes they had fish and, just occasionally, on a Sunday, flesh meat. They worked twelve hours a day and had two days holiday every year, Good Friday and Christmas Day – after they had done the morning's milking!

When the First World War broke out in August 1914, Tom joined the Army. He said: "Our old man had ten lads. We all joined the Army, ten of us, and we all came back at the end of the war! Each one of us was decorated. I should think there is a bit of a record there somewhere, isn't there, Jack?"

One of his brothers though, George, didn't live long after the war. Tom said he had the roof of his mouth shot away and he starved to death in a barn at Ilam. The lady who kept the village shop was the last person to see him alive. She sold him a small loaf. It was with him when he was found.

Old Tom said to me one day: "Ast ever sane the Military Medal, Jack?" I said "No". He said to his wife: "Fetch them medals in out of the front room, Ede." His wife shuffled back with an oak picture frame full of medals. Sure enough there was Tom's M.M. He said: "I get a bit of a pension with it, you know. Tom Walker comes round with it every October – round about my birthday. It used to buy me a couple of ounces of bacca, but nowadays it only buys one ounce!"

He told me of a narrow escape he had in the front line, in France. "I was in a slit trench – there was only room for three of us in it. On my left was an old soldier who had just come back from leave in England. He had married his mate's widow (his mate had been killed in action) and had brought some fags back with him. On my right was a young lad who had not been in the front line before. The old soldier gave me a fag; the boy didn't want one but we persuaded him to have one to steady his nerves. We all lit up – then Jerry dropped a mortar bomb, quite a distance behind us. Soon after he dropped another, 'bout the same distance in front of us. I knew he was ranging us, and I put my arms round the old soldier and the boy and pulled them down into the slit trench with me – it was harldy deep enough for us to stand up in and be covered completely. The next thing I knew was that I was there alone – the fag still in my fingers. The old soldier lay out in no-man's land cut into three pieces. He was cut off at the fork of the arms and at the fork of the legs. The boy was killed too. I put my hand to my face to see if there was any blood – there wasn't a spot. All I had was a nick above the eyebrow, just as if you'd ketched it wi' your thumb neel."

Later in the war Tom was taken prisoner – he was starved again of food. He was released in 1918, the year the war finished, and came out of prison camp on Whit Sunday. Typical of the soldiers of the First World War, he had a big bushy moustache – like America Jack's! When he had finished a cup of tea, old Tom would squeeze his moustache with his hand for the last few drops!

Another Tom, Tom Walker, who I have just mentioned above, kept the garage at Denstone and lived at the Tavern with his three unmarried sisters and aged mother. She remembered the ford at Denstone when the open brook ran across the road near the Tavern. Tom was one of the few people who served in both world wars, 1914–18 and 1939–45 and he was a survivor of Dunkirk.

At Denstone, of the two pubs, the Tavern only had a beer licence, but the Oak had a beer and spirits licence. The Oak and its many outbuildings have long since disappeared, although it out-survived the huge old oak tree from which it derived its name; likewise the adjacent Oak Farm and Oak Lane. This huge tree stood on the corner between

Tom Walker at outbreak of World War II

The Tavern, Denstone, before World War I

The Tavern – present day

the War Memorial and the Oak. It was felled because it had become unsafe.

Mr Green, the landlord of the Oak, an excellent joiner, made a large housekeeper's cupboard out of some of the wood. I remember seeing this piece of furniture at Oak Farm.

The owner of Oak Farm was Harry Chamberlain with his wife Hilda (a good cowslip wine maker). Harry very generously gave a large piece of the best field on his farm to Denstone village on which to build their village hall, and make a car park.

I must record the story of one of my father's old customers here at Denstone. Mrs Edwards lived with her single daughter, Alice, at Rose Bank, near Cromwell's Green. Mrs Edwards, Fanny Lorena Edwards came to live here with her parents at the age of three, and she lived for ninety years in that cottage. She celebrated her one hundredth birthday in 1936 and died in 1937. Born in the reign of King William IV, her long life included Queen Victoria's reign of sixty-four years. She died in the reign of King George VI. She had been born at nearby Stubwood and her father, Samuel Heming, was a fishing tackle maker.

She recalled the marvellous sight of the huge fields of golden corn which grew on the hill opposite her cottage, as they rippled and shimmered in the sun and breeze, before Denstone College was built on these same fields. Even at this great age the old lady could still read without the use of glasses. Two uncles of Mrs Edwards had also lived at Denstone and became centenarians!

Some customers called me Jack, most of them called me John. The ones who called me Jack were mostly older people who knew my father and grandfather – who were both called Jack! Mr Birch lived at Mount Pleasant; his single daughter Jessie 'kept house' for him, his wife having died some years before. I called with bread one day and Jessie was out. The old man said: "Jessie's gun ite – dun yer know what fert lave, John?" I put the bread on the table and Mr Birch said: "What dun way oew thee?" I said: "Oh, Jessie will pay me on Monday." "Nay lad – ah'll pee thee nah." I told him and he paid me, then he said: "Dun yer know what my old dad used fert see? The shortest reckonings make the longest friends." How true!

Mrs Edwards of Denstone – Centenarian

I was amused one day when I took bread to the house, where Jessie the daughter had just put dinner on the table. She asked me if I had seen her father anywhere as she had shouted him for his dinner, but had no response. I said I had seen him in the orchard, and she asked me if I would tell him as I returned to the van. I did so, and her father, Mr Birch, replied, "Aye, let her call agen; it meks yer look so much like pigs if yer goo a-runnin as soon as the bucket rattles!"

Retired from farming at Crakemarsh, Mr and Mrs Prince lived in a bungalow which they had built on the outskirts of Uttoxeter. Old Mrs Prince loved gardening and she would strike cuttings of gooseberries, red and black currants, etc and when they had made nice little bushes, she would often have one waiting for me on my Saturday call. Old Mr Prince would often inquire, "An yer bin to Crakemarsh todee, John?" "I went yesterday." "Did y' say our Billy; as ee dun is eemaking yet?" Mr Prince never smoked in the house – his wife didn't like it. He would always go to the gate for his pipe of tobacco.

The mention of smoking brings to mind the farm labourer who lived at Crakemarsh. He and his wife lived in the farm cottage and his wife worked at the farm, in the house. I called at both places. He was very fond of Park Drive cigarettes and would ask me to bring some on each journey, but his wife wasn't to know! He would leave his money behind a gatepost where I would leave his cigarettes – not such an easy operation as might at first be imagined, as the gate post was in view of the farmhouse and the cottage!

Mr and Mrs Jones lived in the gardener's cottage at Springfields. Mr Jones was gardener to William Bagshaw at the big house. Quite often Mr Jones would give me a bundle of plants, cabbage, cauliflower or brussels sprouts, each in its own season. All were properly wrapped up and 'just right' for planting out.

On Saturdays I would get to Mrs Lowe's about one o'clock. She kept a small place opposite the Church, called Church Farm. Mrs Lowe was the very essence of happiness and good nature. She would say: "Come on, John, you're a bit late. I've put your sausage and chips out. Go in the dairy and cut yourself some bread while I pour out." In the warmth of her kitchen there was always some farm stock being reared. Chickens, ducklings, perhaps a few piglets. I remember one year when half the small kitchen cum living room was fenced off with wire netting and a flock of turkey poults were kept there until they were quite big birds! On one occasion as I drew up on the road outside her house, Mrs Lowe came running out: "Is Jack (her husband) still there?" she asked. I said: "No, he's just got on the Potteries bus." "Oh dear," she said, "he's going to a funeral and I've forgotten to tell him where he is going to!"

Just behind Stramshall Church is a big house. There is about fifty yards of steep gravelled approach to it. Here lived the two Miss Barnwells and their aged bedridden mother. Miss Esmie was the eldest, she was tall and very thin. Miss Violet was short and quite plump. They were the unmarried daughters of the Reverend Barnwell, Vicar of Stramshall for over fifty years. He came from Glastonbury in Somerset. The old thorn tree growing in Stramshall Churchyard, near the Church door, was grown from a cutting off the famous Glastonbury Thorn – this thorn tree which flowers around New Year's Day is said to be derived from the staff of Joseph of Arimathaea who, according to legend, founded the first Christian Church in England.

The Glastonbury Thorn in the centre of the picture

The two old ladies Miss Violet and Miss Esmie lived in the past, in the days when people bowed and courtsied to them in the village. They never accepted modern times and changes and still called their gardener cum handyman by his surname – Adams! The postman would deliver their mail in a leather bag and if they had any to post, it was handed to him in another leather bag. They didn't use public post boxes! Likewise when they travelled, the bus would set them down at their gate and also pick them up at the gate – of course, they would not use the public bus stops!

Delivering bread here was quite a long job – trudging up the rising gravelled drive then climbing a flight of about twenty brick steps before arriving at the back door. I wonder if anyone ever used the front door? I always took a good selection of bread in my basket to try and avoid another return trip to the van. After ringing the bell they would finally arrive at the door to make their joint decision. One of them might ask if I had a plum loaf (a currant loaf); this meant a return to the van and back again, during which time they would have decided to have a plain sponge cake! Down and back again, often in pouring rain; oh well, the customer is always right, and if they aren't, we let them think they are!

Saturday was pay day here, when they paid for the week's bread. When told the amount, one of them would set off to fetch the money, up two flight of stairs – it was never handy or ready – returning with it in a paper envelope. The contents were tipped out onto a table in the passage, the required sum being counted twice by them before being handed over. They never used old or worn 10/– or £1 notes, only new ones from the bank and they would not accept a much used or unclean note in their change. One always had to keep a very clean 10/– note on one side in case it was needed for their change!! In these days £5 notes were seldom ever seen or used, they were white and the writing on them was in black; they were as thin as tissue paper but quite strong. They were the equivalent of a week's wage for most people!

When the two Miss Barnwells made one of their regular visits to local houses and farms – and they walked miles – they were always treated like Royalty and they would generally arrive around tea time!

Townend Farm at Beamhurst was kept by some old men, three unmarried brothers, Cope was their name. One Saturday night (this call was on the last lap of the Saturday rounds), one of the old men was working in the yard with a yellow glimmer of light from a hurricane lantern. I said: "You're working late tonight, Mr.Cope." He replied: "Arr – I like workin' of a nate – you can only say one job as wants doin' at a time!"

Mr and Mrs Ted Sale kept a wood yard in London. They were bombed and the wood yard destroyed in the Blitz of 1942 so they returned to their native district, living at Cherry Tree Cottage, Stubwood. Monday afternoons they always kept me a plate of pudding by, usually either apple or rhubarb. "Put plenty of sugar on it – we don't use it," they would say. Sugar was a scarce commodity and still rationed until the early fifties.

I could go on for ever with these stories, as each one brings to mind another. Let me tell you about old Jim Motteram whom I have mentioned earlier. Jim was an old soldier who served with the Uttoxeter Volunteers, before the turn of the century. He suffered and survived an amazing catalogue of injuries during the 1914 to 1918 war. Wounded by rifle bullets and also shrapnel from shells, he still had shrapnel in his body. He was gassed and also run through by bayonets in several parts of the body including his legs. Jim told me that the first man to be killed in this war from Uttoxeter, was Jimmy Nuttall. They were side by side in the line when they were attacked by the Prussian Guards. Jim said that one of these cut Jimmy Nuttall straight down through the head with his sword. Old Jim was a most kind and gentle person and lived until his nintieth year.

Mrs Jennings at Bramshall was brought up by her great uncle and great aunt. Their names were Cope and she called them Uncle Cope and Auntie Cope. They kept the New Inn at Bramshall. The roads and lanes were all so rough and muddy that everyone wore 'pattens' to go to Church. Mrs Jennings said that pattens were iron hoops worn under shoes and strapped on to them to keep the wearer raised up above the muddy roads! It must have been quite difficult walking in them.

Sand was used a great deal for scrubbing tables and forms to keep them clean and white; sand was also used for washing up. This was before the days of abrasive powders such as 'Vim'.

People had to live by those often quoted lines: "Eat it up - wear it out - make it manage, or go without."

On the Stramshall round I always had my sandwiches at 'Granny' Walker's. Some people called her Nurse Walker, but she was more generally known as 'Granny'. She had been a nurse and midwife in the area for over 50 years and now lived with her husband Joe in retirement, both in their eighties. They were the same age, born in 1870. The Co-op breadman, Tim Deaville, also had his break here but he called on a different day. As soon as I got there, Granny Walker would say, "Sit thee dine i'th rockin' cheer, I'll brew a cup a tay." Old Joe had been a farm worker all his life and even now went to Uttoxeter doing part time work at a chemist's shop, unpacking cases and such like. Granny Walker came from the Grindon area, 'up country' as we call the high ground in the north of Staffordshire. Her dad was a worker on the new railways, labouring and laying the tracks. She told me one day, that their cottage had no lavatory at all. When I enquired how they managed, she said that they "took a walk down the faylds!"

When Granny Walker died, old Joe went to Bramshall to live with his daughter Fanny. I often saw him on his walks and would stop and have a chat with him. One day I was running late and saw old Joe. I passed him by in the van, thinking he wouldn't notice me. Next time I saw him he was most concerned and said: "John, dunna yow ever goo past may agen - you munna ever do that agen." So I was quite rightly put in my place!

Christmas Eve would be the last delivery before the two, or later, three days holiday. This meant that more or less everyone had to have a final call - on all the rounds - so of course this was a very busy day. Extra bread would have to be made, also the additional Christmas fare such as pork pies, mince pies, cakes, etc. We would get the larger items out before Christmas, such as Christmas cakes and plum puddings, often ending up short of bread and having to bake more at night and then go out and deliver it. This often meant being out until well after midnight.

People waited up; it generally fitted in with their time schedule for playing Santa Claus anyway! They all knew that I should turn up sometime - in quite a merry state too, as you might well guess! What a mixture; a glass of rum, coffee, whisky, tea, home made wine and other drinks – all day long!

One Christmas Day I was checking through my bread book in the morning and I hadn't made an entry for Jack and Mary Griffin of Trafalgar House. I had to go and ask them, just to make sure I had called with their bread. When I arrived they laughed and said: "Yes, you called, but we didn't think you knew much about it!"

New Year's Day was not a holiday then and I would be expected to 'let the New Year in' for my customers. This entailed entering by the back door, bringing in the bread and a piece of coal. Then we would have a glass of wine and a mince pie, wishing each other a Happy New Year. I would then leave by the front door.

CHAPTER ELEVEN
Coping with winter

Looking back, the winter's weather not only seemed much worse than it is nowadays – it was worse. A bitterly cold north-east wind would blow for most of the winter and well into spring, giving rise to the saying: "If the wind's in the east on New Year's Day, it will stop there till the end of May." It often did, too!

For bread delivery, in fact for all our outdoor work, Don and myself always wore a white cotton jacket (called a 'slop') and corduroy trousers. When there was a day's heavy rain we wore an oilskin coat and hat. These were heavy but at least they kept the rain out. Cord trousers always gave off an unpleasant smell when they were wet, just as they did when new, and it took many washes before this smell was eradicated! I always wore hob-nailed boots, which I had re-nailed before the leather sole was touched. One of the two important requisites of life – I was told – a good pair of boots, the other being a good bed, because if you are not in one, you are in the other during life's journey!

We did our best to keep the bread dry in the basket by covering it with a tea cloth or by unbuttoning the bottom two or three buttons of the oilskin coat and using one of its flaps as a cover. To deal with snow, floods and other bad weather, of course, we always wore wellingtons. Heavy snowfalls meant that we had to carry a shovel and a bag of gravel, the latter being useful as heavy ballast to keep the back end of the van down as well as for scattering under the wheels to obtain a grip!

On one particular occasion I encountered a big drift of snow at Stubwood. Much higher than the van, a way had been cut through it for a vehicle. It was only when I was half way through that I discovered that the cutting was not wide enough for my van! I wedged to a stop, so I got the shovel, but of course could not open either of the cab doors in the wall of snow. I had to get the shovel out the window and cut away in order to open a door and get out. Of course most of this snow came in the cab – there was nowhere else for it to go! I well remember after making several more calls, one woman said to me: "You're a bit later today, Jack."

One of the worst snows of this century was the first

winter of the war, 1940. I was still at school. I well remember my Dad borrowing a horse-drawn sledge and delivering bread with this at Bramshall. He borrowed it from Statham's farm. I wonder if it is still there? The winter of 1947 was also severe, although I was still abroad in the Army and did not return to England until spring of that year. During this severe snowfall, the road was blocked at the stone wall, Crakemarsh. My Dad got this far with his van loaded with bread. He parked it here and walked back to the Bakehouse. His customers walked to the van, took their bread and left the money and made their various ways home. He fetched the van later in the day and repeated the operation when and where necessary. Everything had been done in a proper manner and the money was all correct and untouched!

It amazed me how the old van would go through snow. I arrived at the railway crossing at Crakemarsh when there had been a good snowfall. Maggie, who lived there said: "You'll never get any farther, John." I could not turn round there anyway, so she opened the railway gates for me and there was a perfect pattern of the gate on the drift filling the lane in front of me! But the van went through it slowly but surely!

CHAPTER TWELVE
More customers and characters

The majority of my customers asked me not to knock on their doors – "just walk straight in", they insisted. "If we are doing anything wrong, then that is our fault, not yours," they would say! But I would always give a knock and then walk in.

Easter was a very busy time, having to make and deliver all those thousands of hot cross buns. Peoples' appetites for these buns seemed insatiable and we could not make enough. They were so cheap too. I used to take them out on my bike when I was at school. They were seven for three pence then. Hot cross buns were only made for Good Friday. Nowadays there are as many sold on Easter Saturday as on Good Friday. With older people it was a tradition to eat these buns for breakfast on Good Friday. Every house seemed to have a couple of dozen at least – oh, the work in them, I dread to think of it even now! The smell of the bunspice permeated your clothes and even your body.

Traditionally we always hang a hot cross bun on a string in the bakehouse, changing it on the following Good Friday for a bun of the new year's vintage. This hot cross bun never gets mouldy. Some bakehouses also keep the old bun and have rows and rows of buns going back many years! Let me point out that this is a tradition and not a superstition!

I always did a few calls in Uttoxeter on my way out to the country rounds. Mr and Mrs Ernie Boot lived in Holly Road. One Saturday they had gone out, leaving the bread tin by the back door. In it was a two shilling piece to pay for the week's bread, which came to one shilling and ten pence halfpenny. I left the bread and three halfpence change and continued on my rounds. Unknown to me, a burglar followed me at Boot's and ransacked the house. He also took the three halfpence change. When he was caught I had to attend the magistrate's court to say I had left the three halfpence!

In Smithfield Road was a shop owned by Mr and Mrs Harold Chadwick, who lived here with their two children, Harold and Hetty. The children were a bit older than I was, but we often went on outings together to local beauty spots like Cannock Chase. Mr Chadwick worked at the local factory of Bamford's

Agricultural Company. He was a tall, thin man, of very quick speech and fast, nervy reactions. His great fascination was betting on racehorses, in fact, his spare time was taken up by working as a bookie's runner, collecting bets! I could never reconcile this with the fact that this man was the same person who had been a pilot in the Royal Flying Corps during the Great War, it just didn't seem possible! However, this was a fact, proved by a very large photograph of him in his R.F.C. uniform, hanging in the living room! At the outbreak of the Second World War in September 1939, it immediately became the dream and only goal of his son Harold to emulate his father and become a pilot with the R.A.F.

I think it was in 1941 that he joined the R.A.F. and was soon accepted as a candidate for pilot training. Harold went to Canada along with his school friend Neville Crisp, nicknamed 'Spud'. There they trained together in the British Empire pilots' training scheme.

No sooner had training begun when Harold discovered he had a disability – he suffered from air sickness and nasal bleeding. He realised that if this continued he would not be able to meet the stringent medical criteria required for a potential pilot. His instructors said he would probably soon settle down and overcome this handicap. To his dismay he didn't, but managed to keep it under wraps – his own personal secret. Despite the dreadful discomfort of flying with his helmet containing vomit and blood, he completed the course.

Harold and Spud were due to receive their 'wings', the coveted badge which would be sewn onto their tunics. Unfortunately, only a week before the presentation at the passing out parade, Harold's closely guarded secret was rumbled and he was disqualified from receiving his wings. His world collapsed and he was returned to his depot in England. Still intent on air crew he decided to train as a bomb aimer. The badge of a bomb aimer was a single wing with the letter 'B'.

Harold got it, and was soon on operations over Europe, lying in the belly of the aircraft, alone, with all the anti-aircraft shells and flak coming up straight at him. He lived against all odds, having flown on the raids to the German dams with 617 Squadron, the Dambusters.

He returned to Uttoxeter after the war; maybe Harold didn't get his wings but he had been awarded the Distinguished Flying Cross for his bravery. His squadron commander, Group Captain Leonard Cheshire, VC helped Harold to start up in a wholesale business in Nottingham, where he lived with his wife Cynthia. He came to see me at the stall in Uttoxeter market at this time. He was very nervy and shaky. His business venture was most successful and happily they soon retired. They went to Spain to live for the rest of their lives. Keeping a smallholding near the Pyrenées, they looked after all kinds of stray, sick and unwanted animals.

Harold's great friend 'Spud' Crisp was killed during the war. Neville Crisp was returning to England, along with several other planes, after a raid on the German-occupied Low Countries. Their planes, Beaufighters, were flying just above the waves coming back over the English Channel. When they reached England, Neville's plane was missing – none of the others had seen it go down, or seen anything unusual. His name is on the R.A.F. memorial at Runnymede, which is dedicated to all R.A.F. personnel without a known grave. Neville's father, a Customs and Excise officer, told me the following story, but was most insistent that I should realise that neither he nor his wife were superstitious.

"One morning a robin came (considered by many to be an omen of ill luck) and spent most of the morning flitting about on the kitchen window sill. At dinner time we went into the dining room to have our dinner, which was our usual routine. The robin then came onto the window sill of the dining room. Several days later we were informed of Neville being missing, presumed killed.

Thinking back, we then realised that Neville's loss was at the same time as the robin's visit – though there could not have been any possible connection between the two events."

Don's mother lived in Park Avenue. There was always a really good cup of coffee here. All milk (sterilised), it was a grand warmer on a winter's day. Nearby lived Walter Underhill, pronounced locally as 'Wotty Undrill". He would often be in the Cock at Beamhurst, enjoying a pint of beer. He was a foreman over gangs of men who repaired the roads. Wotty had the upright stature and looks of a military man, with his sharp eyes, moustache, clean appearance and well-kept boots.

He had, in fact, been a soldier in the Boer War at the turn of the century, and also in the Great War. The father of a large family, he enjoyed going out with the gun to supplement his wages. A good shot, Wotty was an inveterate poacher!

In his later years I would often see him out with his bike as usual, but, unbelievably converted, carrying his binoculars instead of his gun! I remember him saying, "Eh, John, isn't nature wonderful?"

The shop which we now have at The Wharf was owned and kept for about forty years by Mr and Mrs Tom Yates. He was a first war veteran and had a large retail milk round in Uttoxeter. Mrs Yates kept the shop always spotlessly clean; in her blue linen dress with a snow white apron and a white head band, she reminded me of a nurse. I supplied her with bread which was bought in 'stones', there being eight loaves to a stone, with each loaf weighing 1lb 12oz – this made fourteen pounds, or one stone. (I also supplied Chadwick's shop with bread which they also bought in stones.)

Mr and Mrs Yates ran a most successful business, but unfortunately they had no family. One day when I called, Mrs Yates said: "We are retiring soon, John. We have bought a house with a nice garden. I have always wanted to grow roses." Impossible as it seemed for this diligent couple to finish work, they did in fact retire. I would sometimes meet them on their country walks. Mrs Yates grew her roses and saw them flower, but she died quite suddenly soon afterwards. Not long after her death Mr Yates gave us all another surprise by marrying a spinster. It was not long before he, too, passed away and his new wife ended up with the house and all that Mr and Mrs Yates had made in a lifetime of hard work. Such is life!

Before I left the town for the country deliveries, I always filled up with petrol at New Road Garage. This was a big shed made of corrugated iron sheets, with petrol pumps which were wound by hand. It was built and owned by Mr Shaw, a large man with a sharply pointed and waxed moustache. This type of moustache was still quite common, each end of moustache being pulled along and twisted into a sharp, stiff needle-like point with the aid of a wax, specially prepared for this purpose. He loved to use flowery language and big words, quite often in the wrong place, whilst he was pumping the petrol! He let the garage to various tenants over the years but eventually he returned to it himself and he ran it very efficiently. We called him 'Waxy'. He never used banks; he kept his money in cocoa tins, and eventually retired to Bournemouth!

One Monday I paid him for the petrol and put my wallet down on an oil drum and left it there. Monday was not a 'pay day', most people paying at the week-end for the week's bread. It was a couple of hours before I missed my wallet and recollected where I must have left it, returning straight away to the garage. There it was, still on the oil drum!

At the roadside just behind the garage were two small cottages, long since pulled down now. In one of them lived old Joe Siddles. He was a bachelor and he would do any sort of work he could get. He was a night watchman for years; this entailed sitting in a wooden hut - like a sentry box. In front of it would be a brazier full of burning coals to keep him warm while he watched over building sites and the like. Old Joe had a wooden leg. Very often when I called he would be just getting up from his truckle bed in the little living room and I would pass him his wooden leg to screw it on. It had a black shoe and a sock fixed permanently to it and the wooden leg itself was flesh coloured.

Little old Clara Christian lived at the bow-windowed shop, still there today, opposite the Elite Cinema. Her mother, Mrs Christian, kept this as a sweet shop. Clara was sitting at her table one day with a cup of tea, when somehow I managed to accidentally knock the Bible from the edge of the table. This old and worn book managed to part with most of its many loose leaves as it fell to the floor. What a job I had putting it together again in its rightful order!

At Christmas the Vicar would distribute vouchers to old people so that they could purchase some groceries with them. When Clara got her voucher, she would say: "Would you do me a kindness, Mr. Walker, and go to the chemists and get me a bottle of port wine with my voucher. I don't think the Vicar would mind, do you?" I bet she really enjoyed that drink of port each year!

In Park Street I called on the two Miss Malverns, at Slade Cottage. The elder of the two, Jessie, had been a pianist and music teacher all her life. Amy, the younger of them, had been an artist in connection with the advertising trade. They had come to Uttoxeter in the 1920s with their father who was a Methodist Minister. Previous to moving here they had been in Doncaster, but did not like it there – they said the atmosphere was oppressive because Doncaster was below sea level.

They often talked to me about Grandpa. He was their father's father who was a Methodist missionary to the Fiji Islands. The Fijians were all cannibals when Grandpa and his young wife went there to try and convert them to Christianity. At one time his wife had a narrow escape from being killed and eaten. After years of struggling, this devoted couple actually converted all the tribes from cannibalism to Christianity. Before they left Fiji, they persuaded the old tribal chieftain to cede the islands to Queen Victoria. When the missionary couple boarded the boat to leave, the islanders waded as far out into the sea as they could and the chieftain made Grandpa a present of the wooden bowl from which they used to eat the human flesh. According to Fijian custom, when a present was given another present had to be given in return. This caught Grandpa unawares and after a bit of quick thinking, he gave the chieftain Grandma's parasol! Their last view of him was of the old fellow jumping up and down in the sea, laughing for all he was worth and opening and closing the parasol!

The two Miss Malverns had the wooden bowl on their sideboard. I remember it well – quite an intricate piece of work. The whole article was carved out of one piece of wood, yes, even the twisted stem and the base. The dish itself was quite thin, and in its centre a small knob had been left with a hole bored through it from one side to the other. I don't know what its purpose was – neither did they – but it did not drain the dish. It was solid and was about sixteen inches in diameter.

My first call after leaving the town was at Mr and Mrs George Barlow's. They lived with their family of four in some old railway carriages; two were used as bedrooms, one as a living room and one as a store. The rooms were kept clean and spotless by Mrs Barlow.

The Fijiian cannibal bowl

She also worked at the bakehouse in the thirties. No house was cleaner than these carriages with their snow white net curtains blowing in the house. The Barlows were agricultural contractors who did threshing with their old steam engine; later they became scrap metal dealers. Beesons lived in these carriages before Barlows. Their business was in casualty animals, mainly horses which had died and these were boiled up to obtain by-products. Uttoxeter people always complained about the smell coming from Beesons' premises!

Across the road from here was 'Titley's Mill'. This was a water driven corn mill. I have been in the mill while it was working and the whole building shook from top to bottom! Old Tom Titley, the miller, had a short leg and wore a boot with a huge block under it about ten inches deep. He had a bushy white beard and a moustache which was burnt brown with cigarettes!

In the mill field was a disused double decker bus. Bill Clarke and his friend Bill Brown lived in this. They slept upstairs and lived downstairs. Bill Clarke was a Uttoxeter Town Councillor. He and his family had lived at Heath House, quite a big residence but he had been evicted by his fellow councillors with a compulsory purchase order and went to live in the bus. I think his fellow councillors did not like his very outspoken views.

Further on I called on Herbert Davies. On market days, old Herbert would be seen going to Uttoxeter with his tin cans, each with a handle and a lid and he would milk cows which had been brought into the market to be sold – others did this too. The milk was a good help to supplement their meagre wages. On Sundays, old Herbert delivered Sunday papers in the district and always rode his bike down the white line in the middle of the road. Not to be recommended today!

Nearby lived Ernie Egerton, a painter and decorator who worked for my grandad, Trevor Forrester at one time. Ernie was a life long fisherman on the River Dove. Born at Crakemarsh Crossing House, his dad used to knit nets. They would net the pool under the railway bridge at Combridge and these trout were a useful supplement to the diet of old Egerton's large family. Ernie's dad worked as a farm labourer for Berrisford of Lowfields, who owned the brook. The netting would be done at dinnertime when the farmer and his family and workers would be indoors!

Here in the hamlet of Spath lived Jack Harvey, a bachelor. All his working life he had been on the railway. He started work on 'The Old Knotty' (The North Staffordshire Railway Company), always cycling to work, and on the day he retired, he put his bike clips round an ash sapling by his back door and never used them again – over the following years I watched the bark of the tree engulf the over expanded clips! Often in hot weather he would give me a glass of water which he pumped from the well. There was no water like this, ice cold, sparkling and clear – it was pure nectar. Jack, like his mother, was a native of Spath. Her grandparents kept a coal wharf on the canal here. Many local people who emigrated to America and Canada went by boat from Spath to Liverpool and thence to the New World.

Charlie Holmes was the only person I did not call on at Spath. His wife had her bread off the Co-op. But I knew Charlie well. He worked at the Bridge Farm, odd–jobbing. He was a roadman all his life and came from a poor family. Charlie told me about one Christmas he remembered as a boy. They had nothing to eat for their Christmas dinner, but early in that same morning a hare ran into the house. His dad quickly shut the door on it and they had their Christmas dinner!

Charlie's length of road which he looked after was about four miles away. He would cycle to it and take his dinner with him. When he had eaten his dinner, he would often go into the fields and fill his empty dinner bag with dried up cow pats for his garden at Spath!

Bridge Farm was kept by 'Ticker', as he was known, who lived with his old aunt. She would occasionally buy a sack of flour or oatmeal from me for her poultry. When I took the bag on my shoulder she would show me into the dairy where she wanted it. One day she asked for it to be put on a shelf which was about six feet up a wall and not very secure either. When I hesitated and enquired if the shelf was good enough, she replied: "Aye! You blokes are all the same – you're men until you've got a job to do and then you're lads!"

As I have mentioned before, Crakemarsh Crossing House was kept by Maggie. She was a model of cleanliness and efficiency. The railway gates were always kept closed to the road and on arrival one gave a pip or a shout and Maggie would come bustling out to open and close the gates. This was all through the day and night and in all weathers. Maggie's husband was killed in the war but she remarried. One day the railway gates were closed to the railway for some reason and Tommy Taft, an engine driver, was driving a goods train down the line from Rocester to Uttoxeter! Maggie heard a tremendous noise and rushed out to find the gates smashed up and the train stopped just beyond. Tommy Taft, an erratic and eccentric sort of fellow, was walking back up the track and called out: "Some firewood for you, Maggie!"

There was a farm labourer's cottage at Combridge for Eaton Dovedale Farm. A family lived here with several small children. The mother then had twins and was very ill. Despite the doctors visits she gradually became worse and her life was obviously in danger. One Monday morning the husband was at home and came out to the van for his bread. I enquired about his wife's health and he immediately became upset. At this same time there were some gypsies there and one of them asked him what was the matter. He told her that his wife had an incurable haemorrhage. The gypsy woman said to him: "Go down the fields, young man, and look in the hedges – you will find the wild rose growing. On the wild rose you will find here and there a big furry growth (robin's pincushions we call these). Pick some of these and stew them in water. Give her a wineglass full of this liquor night and morning." After doing this, the man's wife never looked back and was soon on her feet again and back to normal.

ROBIN'S PINCUSHIONS

CHAPTER THIRTEEN
Denstone

And so on towards Denstone. On the left-hand side of the road was a marshy area with a lot of springs. There stood the old cheese factory, now the site of the huge JCB excavator complex. When this factory was begun, everyone said that no-one could build anything on such boggy ground! This statement was soon refuted when the massive pile-drivers started work on the foundations in the 1950s.

The first house in the village of Denstone was Mr and Mrs Boot's. They had ten boys and one girl. It would be about eleven o'clock when I got here and Mrs Boot would be peeling a bucketful of potatoes for their dinner. The house was always kept spotless.

Mr and Mrs Frank Parker lived a bit farther on. They had a red and white tin plate on their house wall, 'Trent Parcel Agency'. All buses would carry parcels on their journeys for a small charge in those days – a most prompt and efficient service. In Uttoxeter, the parcel agency was in the Market Place, where the Midland Bank is now at a shop owned by Frank Shaw, brother to 'Waxy' at New Road Garage. The sign outside the shop read 'RF Shaw – Ladies and Gents Outfitters'. He was an eccentric known by the nickname of 'Ta-Ta' (pronounced as it is used in everyday speech for 'good-bye' or for a child's walk.) Perhaps he had been a tailor in his younger days. His appearance was always the same; several tape measures around his neck, pincushions hanging around on cords and several cardigans, all in various stages of disrepair, the pockets bulging with chalks! The shop was full of second hand clothes and witty slogans which Ta-Ta had written.

Of course parcels were all paid for by the sender, the recipient only collected them. Sometimes we would need a box of sultanas or lard from our suppliers at Stafford before their weekly delivery. This would be put on the Stafford to Uttoxeter bus. I would go to Ta-Ta's to collect it. "A parcel from Stafford, Mr.Shaw?" "Not yet, John. I will let you have it as soon as it comes." I would not be back at the bakehouse very long before Ta-Ta appeared – pushing his bike – with the 28lb wooden box of goods on his bicycle carrier! He would come in with it and say: "Your parcel's here; there will be a sixpence delivery charge!" Ta-Ta made sure he got a bonus for delivering the goods as well as for sending them! His bike was his constant companion. When not engaged in parcel deliveries, he would be seen with a narrow spade tied to the crossbar and a box of ferrets on the carrier – off on a poaching expedition – tape measures, pincushions and all! So much for the parcel services.

At Denstone Vicarage lived the Reverend and Mrs Berrisford Smith. They had been in charge of a parish on the Canadian Prairies in their younger days. Mrs Berrisford Smith was a 'local girl', Mary Watson, and was a lot younger than he was. The Vicar's hobby was poultry and he kept grey and white speckled hens called Cuckoo Marans. These laid a very handsome rich deep brown coloured egg. The Vicar and his wife showed me a pair of barn owls one day which had nested there. They were sitting on a branch of a pine tree with their four young ones.

Denstone Village

Nearby lived Mr and Mrs Geoff Byron, farmers. Geoff and Alice Byron, who celebrated their Diamond Wedding, were as 'local' as it is possible to be. Geoff's parents and grandparents – also Alice's parents and grandparents – all lived on farms within a few hundred yards of each other! And amazingly their only son, John, and his family are there now. One day my Dad killed a couple of pigs for them. They had a good dry cellar here and my Dad had one of the hams for himself. When he had finished salting and cutting up, my Dad asked Geoff if he could leave his ham there in the cellar until he needed it. "By all means, leave it till you want it," Geoff said. Some months later, my Dad wanted the ham, he went down the cellar for it – all that was left of it was the skin and the hock bone with the hook in it! Apparently, Geoff had a ginger and white cat which had discovered a small pane of glass broken in the cellar window. They had often remarked how well this cat looked and how fat it had become! How they all laughed!

Next to Byron's was the Vinewood, a nice house with a southerly aspect. It had a grassy bank which always had the first primroses, violets and celandines in Spring. Vinewood was a small farm, a thirty yard walk from the lane. I was halfway between the lane and the house one day when I realised that a commotion was taking place. Mr and Mrs Cope were trying to catch their rough-haired black and white collie dog. It had broken his chain and gone mad. In no time at all the dog spotted me and dragging a few yards of its chain, made a bee-line for me! It was foaming at the mouth. Caught without any cover I used my bread basket to ward off its attacks on me. I must have made one slip-up and the dog got in and bit me on the thick of the leg, above the knee. After this, luckily it made off down the field – Frank Cope after it with his gun. I left their bread and then went next door and asked Mrs Byron if she had any disinfectant. She only had IZAL which she used for the lavatory, so I diluted some of this with water and used it. It cleared up all right, eventually – after going all colours of the rainbow!

Ratcliffe's coal yard as it is now, used to be Faulkner's joiners shop. Old Mr Faulkner was a marvellous joiner and cabinet maker. He made beautiful furniture, mainly in oak. As a hobby he used to make working model ornaments which were operated by the wind. The upright wooden shafts that carried these can still be seen on the shed roof. There were windmills turning round, men chopping wood with axes, a Church with people going inside and coming out through another door, all working perfectly and in brightly painted colours. Old Mr Faulkner had a long white pointed beard down to his waist and always wore his white joiners apron, even when he was digging the garden!

Delivering bread at Troutsdale, near to Faulkner's joiners shop

At Richmond House, Mr Jack Burton lived alone, a retired farmer, with his little Jack Russell Terrier for company. He too had a white beard, but a much smaller one that Mr Faulkner's, a beard more like King Edward's (we nicknamed him 'Bugwhiskers'). When he fetched his money out of his pocket to pay me, I always noticed that there was something like a round stone amongst his change. I asked him what it was one day. He said "Guess!" After several wrong tries he told me it was a potato. He said that as a youth his back gave him so much pain that he was bent over and had to walk with two sticks. Someone told him to always carry a potato in his pocket, leaving it there all the time. He said his back never troubled him again, but he changed the potato several times over the years, as it wore away.

An old widow who used to keep some tea rooms at Alton

Towers, lived at Denstone with her helper and companion, an old spinster. Theirs was a very small kitchen, as the saying is, not big enough to swing a cat around. The only other room downstairs was the small front room, known as the 'parlour' and only used on Sundays when they would finish dinner and wash up before one o'clock, then go into the parlour until nine o'clock. They had a small coal fire in this parlour and everywhere was kept clean and polished. Even the iron fireback behind the fire was kept shiny with grate polish! There was just a narrow strip in the centre where smoke and heat prevented a polished surface. It was the job of the old spinster to put coal on the fire when necessary. The old widow would tell her exactly where to put each piece of coal so that the smoke and heat would be directed as close as possible to the unpolished centre of the fireback!

Sometimes the old spinster would ask if she could listen to the nine o'clock news on the radio. This request would always be refused, as it was time to close the parlour for another week. This entailed opening out old newspapers and spreading them all over the chairs and table. They lived here together for years – in amicable disagreement!

In a small one room up and one room down, cottage in Oak Lane lived Miss Bott. The walls of her room were decorated all over with newspaper and magazine pictures of the Royal Family, from Queen Victoria onwards. There were even written articles cut out and pasted up on the walls. The room was full up with furniture, baskets, old newspapers in piles, dried flowers and bric-a-brac. As you went in from the door there was just a single track round the circular table. This table was also covered in pots and pans, cutlery and papers of all sorts – just a small patch left clear for Miss Bott to eat her meal! There were saucers of milk everywhere on the uneven floor for her army of cats, and you had to be very wary of stepping on a saucer. Miss Bott was a most excellent brewer of homemade wine – what matter if a mouse did occasionally get drowned in the barrel! Did she know that fermentation was a good method of sterilisation? She always walked with a rolling gait, like a sailor. Whether this was due to the wine or not I could never decide! Miss Bott never went grey; her hair was as black as a crow's wing when she was eighty.

Most houses had a salt box, generally on a nail by the

fireplace. No longer in use for salt, this particular antique always seemed to have been handed down and kept as a decoration or ornament. Some were square boxes and others were tapered, but seldom were they alike. These were strong oak boxes, usually with a loose lid and very dark coloured – stained with the smoke of centuries. Each would hold two or three pounds of salt.

Before leaving Denstone, let me recall old Rowbottom. He lived alone in a very small asbestos bungalow; a mixture of hermit, miser and recluse. When

A tapered salt box

he opened his door, there was his camp bed on the floor and all his belongings in piles, a chair with no seat in it and stacks and stacks of old newspapers, OXO tins and jam jars which he had hoarded up over the years! Old Rowbottom always wore a hat, an old yellow straw hat with no crown left in it, just his bald head shining out of the top! When he paid he always turned his back towards me so that I shouldn't see inside his purse! What a character he was!

A steep climb out of Denstone took me next to the small hamlet of Stubwood. Mr and Mrs Bell lived in a cottage here in an orchard. She was a hard working middle aged woman who rode a very high bicycle and worked at Denstone College. Mr Bell was much older, a very old man. Their living room had bare brick walls and a brick floor; everywhere was always scrubbed out clean but very sparsely furnished, and they would each sit on a hard wood chair. They always had a good fire but it was freezing cold in that draughty room with its old plank door. Their only comfort was cleanliness!

Mr and Mrs Podmore lived at the other end of Stubwood. He had been married twice and I think he had about six children with the first wife and about ten with the second wife. He had made a life long study of growing kidney beans and would always be willing to pass on any information about the subject to anyone who enquired. Spring and summer were, of course, spent in growing the beans and in winter he would be busy preparing his ground, gathering bean sticks, making seed boxes and making good his small glass 'frames' which were all over the place! Old Podmore would try all sorts of soil, leaf soil or loam, the use of animal manure and artificial manure – or soot. They were grown in sun and shade and all aspects of the compass in his experiments.

Many years ago, my kidney beans had not germinated very well and I asked old Podmore if he would sell me a box of beans, which he did. He enquired about mine and said: "How deep do you set them?" I told him about two inches. "Cum wi' may – I'll show yer how fert set 'em." I followed him through the maze of narrow paths and bean rows, then he showed me some boxes of beans he had set late for more trials. Now followed his instructions: "Never bury the banes – just push the bane into the ground with its eye down and lave it as yer can still say the top o'the bane showin'." How right he was. I still set like this today and germination is assured! "Banes need plenty of waiter when they're in the grane bud stage," he'd say.

Some years, late spring frosts would kill most peoples' beans – old Podmore would do a roaring trade in those years. He could always supply any demands! I knew him to keep bean roots from one year to the following year, like a dahlia tuber, and grow them as part of his experiments! Even different types of sticks and canes were used. He decided that the bean preferred a 'rough hazel stick' to any other stick or cane.

My last call at Stubwood was at George Wheeldon's farm. Watkiss's came to live here after old George finished farming, and George came to lodge with my next door neighbours, Mrs Weaver and her daughter Joan. Old George Wheeldon was one of the quietest and kindest men you could ever meet. It just did not seem possible that he could have lived through such trauma and horror, as a boy of sixteen serving with his regiment, the 'Green Howards' in France during the First World War. These are just a few of the stories he told me of his wartime service with the army.

"I was in the Ypres area for three years. After three

weeks of the German bombardment of Ypres there was not a rat left alive – no, not a rat! I saw all my Company (100 men) killed or severely wounded and replaced by new ones. I lived to see this happen not once but twice. I just don't know how or why I still lived; it didn't seem possible that I should be alive.

"One day the Mayor of Poperinghe, a small town near Ypres, asked our Regiment for help to repair a hole in the road leading to his village. Jerry had blown a tremendous crater in the road, making it impassable. A sergeant was detailed to take a platoon of men (28) to do the job. I was one of them. It was a lovely Sunday morning, the sun was out and you couldn't tell there was a war going on – there was not a sound that morning. We marched there in good spirits, then made a first class job of filling in the crater with stones and soil and some limber wheels and then tamped it down well. When the job was finished we formed up and started to march back. We hadn't gone far when a dreadful feeling came over us, something I can't

George Wheeldon

describe – a feeling of impending death. Nobody spoke much and we marched at a fair pace. Then suddenly a shell went over us – it went PING, as it sped over us.

"The next thing I remember was waking up and I was in the clouds, big white fleecy clouds and I remember thinking that I had died and gone to heaven. You see, John, my idea of heaven was of big white clouds and angels flying about; I was only sixteen, you know. Then I realised that I was lying down on the ground and what I had thought of as clouds was in fact smoke. I was alone and it now came to me that I was in the army and must get up. I tried to stand up but couldn't use my legs. Then I rolled over and tried to get up that way; this time I managed it. I had no idea at all where I was or what had happened, but I knew that I had got to find some cover first of all and then try to get back to our lines – where they were, I had no idea."

"There was a small spinney of sycamore trees nearby. I went there and spent some time trying to decide which direction was North. After making my decision, I started out and luckily went in the right direction and reached our lines. They told me I was the only survivor from the platoon – we must have had a direct hit from another shell after we had heard the first one go over."

"On one occasion Jerry broke through the line; it was near Armentiers. This part of the line was held mainly by Portuguese troops and they were very poor soldiers. We were sent to try and hold Jerry and reform the line. Armentiers was a very big town, you know, John, a town as big as Derby. Jerry had come through quite strong; it was quite a bad breakthrough. I was on a captured German machine gun. We mowed them down like flies; just like flies. Unfortunately, a lot of civilians were killed in that battle, but we stopped him, pegged him down and held the line."

"While I was in France I once got the chance of leave; fourteen days leave in England. Many soldiers didn't go on leave. They were afraid that once they got back to England they would not be able to face a return to the hell hole out in France. They would be tempted to desert, so they just soldiered on. I decided to take my leave and was looking forward to it."

"Just before I was due to come out of the line for this leave, I got a letter from my mother in Tutbury. She said Harry, my younger brother, was now in the Army and had been sent to France and would I look out for him. Poor mother, she didn't realise how many troops there were in France, millions, and of all nationalities! Well, what do you know, a couple of days before my leave I saw a big contingent of troops marching up to the line as reinforcements, and I spotted my brother Harry amongst them! I couldn't believe it! I shouted to him and he seemed to turn his head; whether he heard me or not I don't really know because at that very moment, that very second, a German shell came over and took his head straight off. I knew then that I should see my mother before the War Office telegram, which would officially break the news to her. All the way back to England I was rehearsing exactly what I was going to say to her when she said, 'Have you seen our Harry?' We lived in Tutbury, you know, John, and as I turned the corner by the Leopard, I saw my mother standing by our door."

"When I reached her I started to tell her my rehearsed words, but nothing came out of my mouth; I tried again, and again, but nothing would come. She put her arms round me and took me in the house, sitting me down on a chair, just inside the door. She no longer needed to ask me; she knew. She never got over it, it killed my mother."

Old George used to say: "If you want to live and thrive, let the spiders run alive." He loved Nature and all rural life. Are we able nowadays to appreciate life quite so much as he did?

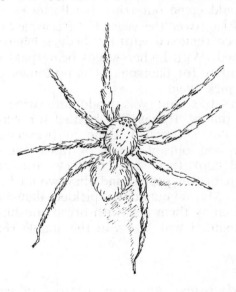

CHAPTER FOURTEEN
Denstone damsons

The district which I have just written about, Denstone and Stubwood, has always been famous for its damsons. Denstone damsons were sought after by all the large fruit markets in England. In spring, the blossom from these prolific trees was like a white froth which had been poured over the landscape, a grand sight. The fruit was a welcome source of extra revenue for everyone, besides being a good standby for winter months. Damsons do not crop well every year, some years there is a glut and other years very few, and of course they fetch a good price in years of scarcity and a very low price when they are in abundance. In good years they would fetch £1 a 'strike'. This was the term used for weighing damsons, a strike being 80lb. If there was a good crop, a person could pick two strikes in a day.

At every farm and cottage there would be damsons in baskets, bath tubs or any other handy container, awaiting the buyers who would come out from the Potteries or Nottingham – even London. Alas, over the years the trees have gone into decay, fallen down, been removed with the hedges where they grew, and generally declined. With higher wages being paid today, even with a much higher price for damsons, it is no longer a viable business proposition to pick them.

This versatile fruit was made into wine, jam and pickle amongst other things. It was also bottled for winter use. Bottled damsons were not necessarily done in preserving jars – these were expensive and out of reach of most country people. My Grandma would cook them and put them into ordinary jars, tie them down with brown paper, and they would keep well into the winter months. My favourite is 'pickled damsons', grand with cold meat, or I enjoy them just with bread and butter for tea. The flavour is exquisite. I will give you the simple recipe:

Pickled Damsons

> *3lb of damsons, 2lb sugar, ½ pint of white wine vinegar, ¼ ounce of cinnamon, 18 cloves*
> *Bring the vinegar, sugar and spices to the boil,*

pour over the damsons and leave to stand all night. Next day, drain off the liquor and bring it to the boil. Then put in the damsons and boil for five minutes. Take out the fruit and put it into warm jars – about ¾ full. Boil up the liquor again and pour it over the fruit – covering it well.

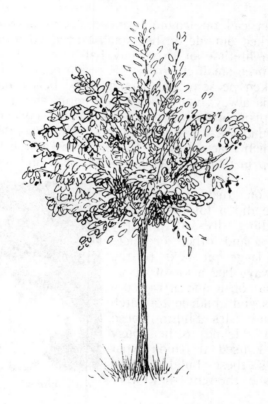

CHAPTER FIFTEEN
The Bramshall round

Every Tuesday and Friday we did the smaller Bramshall round. This ancient hill-top village could only be reached by going uphill from any direction. There were a few thatched cottages in Bramshall.

My first call on leaving Uttoxeter was at Mrs Shipton's farm. She worked outside on her small farmstead in all weathers. She had had a lifetime of extremely hard work, being widowed and left with three small children. She was a most kind, polite and very well spoken person, which completely belied her workaday appearance. She always wore wellington boots and a coarse apron – that is an apron made out of an opened out corn bag and tied with tapes around the waist. Mrs Shipton had a wonderful head of white hair, which reached down to her knees at the back. It was always done up in plaits and coils on her head and was kept very nice.

Being on the outskirts of Uttoxeter, she did a lot of trade at her door, selling dressed poultry, milk and eggs and other produce. There was a large pit next to the farm. This always had a lot of ducks swimming about on it and attracted a lot of mothers and children to watch and feed them. Mrs Shipton bred bulldogs as a sideline to her busy farming life. I used to think what ugly creatures these bulldog pups were – but she thought they were beautiful!

Mrs. Shipton

I am afraid to say that I took advantage of her kind and generous ways. If I had any bread which was damaged, perhaps wet with condensation, overbaked or made unsatisfactory in any other way, I would put it in the basket at Mrs Shiptons. I would of course apologize for it not being up to standard. She would always give me a broad smile as she took the bread and refuse to have any apology, saying it was quite all right and how lucky they were to have bread to eat anyway!

The two Miss Wards lived in a thatched cottage in the village of Bramshall. One of them died and the other lived on alone. She told me something of a secret, when she was nearly ninety. She said: "I was married once, my name really is Mrs Ludbrooke." She and her husband had a small cottage and had only been married a few days when she had to go into hospital to have a cyst removed. She was in hospital several days and could not understand why her husband had not been to see her. Anyway, she returned home and found that he had gone and taken every single thing out of the house. It was empty. She never saw or heard of him again in all her life, and was always known as Miss Phoebe Ward.

In the next cottage, which had a large garden and an orchard, there lived a retired farmer, Mr George Martin. His wife had died and they had no family. They had both come to Bramshall from the Leek area. Old George was exceptionally wealthy but always lived and dressed like a farm labourer. Very frugal in his habits, dressed as a rule in cord trousers and a brown 'milking slop' coat; he wore heavy hobnailed boots. He really enjoyed the deception when people took him for a 'down and out' fellow! He thought nothing about walking to Leek – about twenty miles away. Sometimes motorists or lorry drivers would pick up old George and give him a lift. I remember once a lorry driver put him off at the Three Tuns, Uttoxeter, so that he could walk back home to Bramshall. The driver felt sorry for him and gave him a sixpence – and old George took it! He owned farms and property all over England, but mainly in the Leek and Macclesfield areas.

I laughed one day when he said he'd been into a café at Stafford for a cup of tea and the girl had asked him for the money before she would give it to him! At a sale of property in Cheshire, which consisted of a farm and several cottages and a lot of ground, the auctioneer's clerk, on seeing old George make the final bid, came over to him and asked his name and enquired if he would be able to pay a deposit that same day. Old George replied: "Thay cost have it ow now if thee wants it." He had enough money on him to pay for it outright!

When I called once he was just setting off on his travels

and was folding a piece of currant bread in two, and putting it in an envelope for his waistcoat pocket. He sat on the board of the Commissioners of Inland Revenue for Staffordshire! George always wore a black coat to attend these meetings. Never visiting a dentist, he would go to the doctor for attention to his teeth and pay him for doing it, as people did years ago. George never drew his old age pension. He did not think it was a right and proper thing to do, as he was able to live without it. He was frugal but not greedy. He had been known to rescue some pikelets which had been put on his neighbour's pig churn. He said there was nothing wrong with them and it was a shame to give them to pigs!

When I called on him – Tuesdays and Fridays – he always got me to make him a good saucepan full of porridge and fry him a pan of bacon, so that it would last him until I called again.

Old George never had much fire in the grate and if it did burn up well, he would fetch some garden refuse in and damp it down.

One day, to my surprise, he went to a chest of drawers and fetched out a new land measure in its round leather case. He gave it to me, saying: "The Missus bowt it – it's never bin used – I want you to have it, Jack." I have still got it and it has always been most useful to me. He was a great believer in holly hedges for making a good stock-proof fence, and was always planting them. George left a field of ground to Bramshall Church and hedged this with holly.

Once he went to view an estate which was being sold and the next time I saw him I enquired if he had bought it. His reply contained all the wisdom of a lifetime's experience in property: "Nay, lad, it were all red tiles – I never buy owt wi' red tiles on it."

My next call was at Bramshall station. Here there used to be a platform, waiting room, signal box and station house. This had all gone over the years and the station house was a private house. The people here kept a lot of pigs and also bred dogs. These dogs were mainly chows, with their blue tongues, and large poodles. As soon as I arrived with the van, about twenty dogs would come running to the yard gate. I would enter with my bread basket, taking no notice at all of all these dogs milling around as I went to the back door with the bread. One day,

Bramshaw Church
'96 St Lawrence

Jenny, who lived there, happened to say that one of the big poodles amongst them was quite savage and would not let anyone in, but it never seemed to bother about me for some reason. The next time I went there I recalled this in my mind as I passed through the dogs. Straight away this particular dog, as if it had read my mind – or even noticed a slight hesitation – came and had a go at me, also of course exciting the others. I got to the back door all right but after that I used a roadside door to avoid their intentions!

Mr and Mrs Ben Blore were at the next farm. She was always most polite and well mannered. In summer she would often cut me a bunch of sweet peas for my mother and always put a few sprays of gypsophila with them. An old fellow was laying a roadside hedge for them once, and Mrs Blore had taken him some tea and something to eat. He had put his china cup saucer and plate on the path and of course I put one of my hobnailed boots on it all and smashed it to smithereens! Mrs Blore didn't mind about it at all!

When I had false teeth in the late fifties, old Ben said:

"Never take them out – it doesn't matter how much they hurt and burn – if you once start taking them out, you will never get used to them. If they are really bad, just take them out and put them under the pump and pump some cold water on them and put them back straight away." Excellent advice!

Mr and Mrs Corbishly had a haulage business near the Church, mainly cattle transporting. They had six sons and came from the Mermaid, a pub and small farm on the high moorlands near Leek. Grand old fashioned people. They had a telephone – in these days very few people had phones and they would let anyone in the village use it, if need be. One night a neighbour called and asked Mrs Corbishly if he could use the phone. "Certainly, go in the front room. You know where it is." He went in and had a bit of a shock: In the dim light of the room, old Mr Corbishly was lying dead in his coffin. Mrs Corbishly had forgotten to mention this to him!

One Friday afternoon when I called, Mrs Corbishly wasn't about and this was unusual. As I stood there debating with myself how much bread to leave, I thought I heard her calling me. I ran round to the back of the house and found that she was cornered inside the coal house by their own Alsatian dog. It was a big dog called Bruce. I never liked it and I often warned her about it, although she had had it as a pup. It had a piece of chain on its collar and I managed to get it and lock it in a shed. I think they had it destroyed after this. Mrs Corbishly would have been in her eighties then.

Bert Wheildon was a retired farmer. He also owned quite a bit of property here and there and was quite well off. I met him one day and he asked me if I had seen his trout lakes. I had never even heard of them! We walked down the valley and saw where he had employed diggers to excavate a couple of huge trout lakes. These were fed by springs from the hillside, and the water went from them into Bramshall brook. There was an island in the middle of the largest lake and we walked over a wooden bridge to it. At intervals along the bridge a dead hen would be suspended from a piece of string. Bertie would hit the hen with his stick and maggots would then drop from it into the water. Trout would come and nearly jump out of the water for their treat!

I returned to the bakehouse from Bramshall by way of

Pigeonhay Lane (pronounced 'Pidginny'), a very narrow, winding and picturesque lane. In the hedge, here and there, were one or two big square oak posts. These posts were only as high as the hedge and still retained traces of paint on them from the last century. They were boundary posts, marking the limit of the estate of Lord Willoughby de Broke. He was the Lord of the Manor at Bramshall in the reign of Queen Victoria.

One of my calls was at a cottage in a very isolated place. Built on the edge of a wood, it was at one time a gamekeeper's cottage. Here lived an old lady, rather reclusive and eccentric. She was married to a man over twenty years younger than herself who only came home at weekends. During the week he lived in Birmingham, where he owned a plastics factory and manufactured surgical syringes.

The old lady had in fact been married three times, first to a baker and then to a vicar, before marrying her present husband. There had been a most traumatic ending to the vicar's life. They had a living near Wolverhampton, and one Sunday morning, after the usual service, they decided to go out for their dinner. After setting out in their small car they arrived at their destination, a small pub at the bottom of a short, steep hill. It was an awkward place to park in the pub yard, so the vicar stopped in the road while his wife got out and stood in the pub yard, ready to direct the vicar to reverse into a parking space. At this moment a Pratt's green and yellow petrol tanker came down the hill out of control, crashed into the vicar's car and all were engulfed in flames. Such was the ferocity of the blaze that nothing was left of the vicar's body after the inferno.

The lady had reared several adopted children, but had only one of her own – a son from her first marriage. During the Second World War her son fought in German-occupied France with the resistance movement. He was taken prisoner, and endured captivity in one of the Nazi death camps. After the camp was liberated by British troops he was sent back to Britain to be repatriated. The war was not yet over, of course, and the ship he was travelling on from France to England was torpedoed by a German U-Boat and sunk. Several survived, and in the minutes before the ship went down he was put onto a cork mattress and left on the sea to his fate. His weak and emaciated body, on the cork raft, was washed ashore near to St Nazaire, still alive, but he died soon afterwards and was buried there. His mother often visited his grave.

On approaching the old lady's cottage, one was immediately struck by the tight security system in operation. First there was a couple of locked gates, and then the cottage itself, which had some high poles about twenty feet high around its curtilage. These poles had a wire cable running from the top of each pole to the top of the next one, and along each of these cables ran a lead which dangled down and was fastened to the collar of a large dog! Yes, there was a 24 hour dog patrol in operation! Inside the cottage it was crammed full of beautiful old furniture, china, copper, brass, pictures and other valuables. All were kept in nice condition. There were also guns, one of which had been used by the old lady to scare away an intended intruder on one occasion, during the night.

Despite all her precautions, she was robbed of many thousands of pounds, not by thieves or raiders but by conmen posing as workmen. The old lady decided to have her cottage heated by radiators which were to be warmed by water which had been heated by means of a solar panel on the roof. The 'workmen' came and installed the radiators, the solar panel and a tank in the attic. The system seemed to work out very well, until her next electricity bill came, and apparently the men had simply put an immersion heater in the tank and coupled up to her electricity supply. The 'solar panel' was simply a piece of glass in a frame!

CHAPTER SIXTEEN
The Stramshall round

Let us now make a few calls on the Stramshall round. Leaving Uttoxeter, the first farm would be Mellor's, now pulled down. Several unmarried sisters and brothers lived here, also a lame man with a club foot who had always lived and worked with them. He was always called Tortoishell. He was not related to them at all; in fact he was very distantly related to me! Mellors would have eight or ten loaves at each call and we called three times a week!

The grand residence known as The Parks was the next call. Here lived Mr and Mrs Cyril Bamford, the parents of J.C.B. When Cyril Bamford died, Mrs Bamford, who was Spanish, went to live at Bramshall. Mr and Mrs Roper now came to live at The Parks with their young family. These very pleasant people were pottery manufacturers. The factory they owned at Longton was named 'Tams'. At Christmas, Mrs Roper would give Don and me a half tea service, a gift quite out of proportion to the service we rendered to them! I would often forget to save Mrs Roper's Hovis bread which she liked, putting on her very good nature as seemed to be the usual case.

Allen's farm was the next call. This was a couple of fields away from the road, which entailed opening and closing two gates, sometimes three, quite a time consuming task as it was necessary both going to the farm and returning if stock was about. Here lived old Mr Arthur Allen and his housekeeper, Miss Green. Mr Allen's wife had died forty years before and her sister Sarah Green had looked after Mr Allen and his family from then on. Also living here was Mr Allen's son Walter with his wife and their son.

Allens would have about eight loaves at each delivery. Ten or eleven people would sit down to a meal, including the farm workers and a couple of loaves would be cut up at a meal. Old Arthur Allen presided over all at the table, and ruled with a rod of iron!

Miss Green was quite a character; bare-legged, she wore heavy mens' boots unlaced; on her head she would wear a handkerchief tied with a knot at each of the four corners. When she occasionally went out she would wear a large brimmed black hat which she would polish up with the black lead brush – a brush used for putting black polish ('black lead' it was called) on the grate!

When you went into her kitchen with the bread, Miss Green would meet you and say: "Giz thee baskit" and would take it straight into the dairy and empty it. Then she would come out to the van and decide what to buy, in the cake line. If she spotted any bags of cakes which may have been ordered, she would open them up and look inside, saying: "I'll have these, too." She would accept no defence. If I said: "Oh, they are ordered by Mrs So and So". She would reply, "B....... Mrs So-and-So, I'm havin' 'em!" She would hunt through the van like a weasel, and if we did have to keep any orders on one side for other customers, we had to use the tool box or a similar hiding place. She would even look inside the cab! When she had finished and gone in the house, the young Mrs Walter Allen would then come out and buy what she required. She paid for hers there and then. Miss Green's stuff had to be booked; she paid on Saturday for the week's goods and this was always quite an occasion as you might well guess!

Old Mr Allen was a giant of a man. He would be getting on for twenty stone, with white hair and a big white moustache and red faced; he was how we all picture John Bull, except for the fact that he always wore a brown milking slop instead of the Union Jack! He always cut the sides of his boots, even new ones, before he wore them – to allow his feet to spread out.

I would arrive about five o'clock on Saturdays – tea time. He always paid out the family and farm workers their wages at this time. He would often await my arrival for change so that he could give everyone exact money. I well remember him saying to me on one occasion: "Can you change me a penny for two halfpennies, please, Master John?" He was always polite and well-mannered, blunt but straight to the point and he brooked no nonsense. Miss Green would now say: "Well, what dun way owe thee, Master John?" I would start to reckon up my book and very often Miss Green, who was rather talkative, would have to be silenced by Mr Allen who would say: "Miss Grane, will you please kape your chops shut so as Master John can reckon up his book."

92

At Uttoxeter Smithfield. On the right Mr Arthur Allen, next to him, his son Walter, then Tom Tideswell (neighbour) and on the left, Frank Smith butcher.

In these days, when one is supposed not to eat fat, I often think of old Mr Allen who would eat a plateful of fat boiled ham. When he had eggs and bacon, Miss Green would pour half a pan full of bacon fat over it until everything was swimming in fat! Mr Allen would mop it all up with round after round of bread! He lived until well into his eighties.

When my father was delivering bread, Mr Allen once said to him: "Jack, I have a lot of bread off you. I'm a good customer of yours. I think you ought to let me have my bread a halfpenny a loaf less than you charge me now." At the risk of losing his custom, my Dad said: "Mr Allen, I call on one of your farm labourers down the road. He lives in poor circumstances; he is not well off, as you are, and he always pays me what I ask. It would not be right for me to let you have your bread at a less price than he pays for his bread." Old Mr Allen always respected my Dad for that piece of philosophy.

Before leaving Allen's farm, let me mention a good cure which the old man gave me. I had a couple of warts on my hand, and over the course of a few years these warts slowly increased in number until I had perhaps forty of them, some of them barely visible, up to my elbow. People would tell me all kinds of weird cures and I tried them all – but to no avail! My Dad had the ability to 'charm' warts, but it didn't work on me. People would go up to him and show him their warts. He would look at them, that was all. No word was spoken, not even 'thank you'. Jessie Birch was a young lady at Denstone who played the cello. She had warts on her hand which interfered with her plucking the cello strings. She showed them to my Dad and they disappeared.

But let me tell you of a few 'certain cures' for warts which I tried before getting Mr Allen's cure:

Count the warts (very difficult with mine), tie this many knots in a piece of string then throw the string into a pit or a pond, and as the string rots away so the warts will go.

Steal a piece of raw beef, rub the warts with it, don't tell anyone you have done it or let anyone see you do it, then, same again, throw it into a pond or a pit.

Moisten the red end of a match and rub the warts with it twice a day.

Get a black slug and rub the warts with this, then stick it on a blackthorn in the hedge, and as it rots so the warts should disappear!

Pull one of the succulent petals off a house leek and squeeze the drop of green juice out of it on to the warts every day. (The house leek is the cactus-like plant which grows in clumps on old tiled roofs.)

Anyway, so much for all these cures – none worked with me – until one day old Mr Allen noticed them. "Are those warts on your 'ands, Master John?" "Yes, Mr Allen." "Well, I'll tell you 'ow to cure 'em. Rub 'em wi' caster oil every nate and every mornin' – it'll cure warts on 'osses and cows, so it'll cure 'em on you, Master John." I thought to myself, "here we go again", but I was wrong – it did cure them, even those which I couldn't hardly see. They all disappeared!

My next call was at Ede's farm. This was a grand farm,

run and kept in perfect condition by the family. In the kitchen, the chairs, table and forms were all taken out and scrubbed every week – they were snow white, like the ceiling and walls. Edes had ground on both sides of the busy main road, and when cows were brought across the road to be milked or taken back again after milking, all the family turned out. They held traffic up and marshalled the cows across; woe betide any hapless young motorist who tried to edge past or even negotiate the cows. He would receive, quite rightly, the sharp edge of Mrs Ede's tongue! No sooner were the cows safely across than all the family turned out again with brushes and shovels to clean the muck off the road because of its danger to vehicles – there was a slight bend in the road here, more sharp than it appeared at first sight.

Mrs Ede had quite a big family. One day she told me this story: She had two or three children and was preparing them for school. She was expecting another child and thought to herself: "I will tell the children first before it becomes generally known, as this is the right thing to do." She said to them: "We are going to have another baby, not that it is any secret really, but I wanted you to know first, although I don't want you to go about making it known to everyone." They became very quiet and just before they went off, one of them, Charlie, said to his mother: "Does my Dad know?"

A couple of strangers came to live in a cottage near here, perhaps cockneys, but certainly not local people. I had called on them for some weeks when, as I approached the cottage on one of my calls, I thought I saw a child at the bedroom window, the child moving out of sight very quickly as if it had been snatched to one side. I was not really sure of this but my thoughts were confirmed when I arrived at the farm, only a hundred yards away. As soon as I got there, Mrs Reeves said: "An yer sane a chilt at the cottage up the lane?" I told her what I thought I had seen and said to her: "Leave it to me." This was of course before all the present day armies of social workers. I rang my own doctor, Dr Coventry, from the next phone box. He was soon on the job. The child was a girl of about nine. Luckily she had not been physically ill treated, although mentally so, by being kept at home by her parents who were it turned out semi-deficient, mentally.

This Mrs Reeves who lived at the farm was talking about

teeth one day and told me that hers were made of gold. She took them out and showed me them. Sure enough the whole roof of the top set was in solid gold. I've never seen or heard of the like, before or since! I think she had a gold tooth as well, although I'm not really sure of that, but they must have cost a fortune!

Mrs Reeves had been a widow for years and her two unmarried brothers had lived with her. One of them, Archie, had died but Dick was still living there. Dick had been mentally unstable all his life but was a very good and conscientious worker. Quite often he would become annoyed with people around him and start shouting, swearing and cursing at the top of his voice. He would then make off towards Stramshall, cursing loudly all the way until he got to Mrs Lowe's at Church Farm. She would take him in and talk to him, giving him a cup of tea and he would soon be all right again. Mrs Reeves always knew where he could be found – at kind-hearted Mrs Lowe's! He would be back to normal then for a few more weeks!

'The Park'
Stramshall
'96

Nearby lived old Herbert Reeves, father-in-law to Mrs Reeves. There were three gates to open at this farm! Herbert Reeves had been a successful farmer, cattle breeder and judge of cattle. He told me that when he left home, his father gave him a calf and a gold sovereign. His unmarried daughter Edith kept house for him. When it was butter-making day, Miss Reeves would always put out a glass of buttermilk for me when I called, adding a pinch of salt. Every Saturday Mr Reeves would pay for the week's bread with a cheque, always using a blue lead pencil and often his signature went off the cheque before he had finished it! But the bank always accepted it! Tall, and straight as a ramrod, wherever he walked on the farm he always carried a 'thistle spud'. This is a five foot hazel stick with a 1½ inch blade hoe on the bottom end of it, for chopping off thistles and weeds, whenever they were seen in the fields. Old Herbert was active until he died, just three months before his hundreth birthday.

One of his many children, Harry Reeves, kept a woodyard and farm nearby. Harry's wife asked me if I would make a wedding cake for her daughter Nancy. When details of the cake were arranged, Mrs Reeves asked me if I would use a small bottle of rum in its making. I told her that I would. The next time I called she gave me two bottles of rum, saying: "There's one for the cake and one for you, otherwise you would end up drinking most of the bottle and using hardly any for the cake!"

My next call was at the gate lodge to Beamhurst Hall, Mr and Mrs Sears. He was a gardener at the Hall and his wife bred wire-haired terriers. These beasts were really savage and were often loose! The procedure here was to go to the garden gate en route for the back door and wait at the gate for a few moments. If Mrs Sears was in she would come to the gate and take the bread, the dogs barking in attendance. If she was out, all would be quiet and the dogs could be heard barking in the house. Then you went through the gate and round the house to the back door, where a bread tin was left.  One particular day I waited at the gate - nothing stirred - I went round the house, and just as I got to the back door I noticed the door was open a couple of inches, and no tin was left out. As I quickly made a dive to close the door, two wire-haired terriers beat me to it. Both got their noses through the narrow gap and bounded out at me, one above the other. They both bit me at the same time, one just above the knee and the other just above that one! Mrs Sears then appeared, got her dogs back inside and gave me a good 'telling off' for swearing. So I lost out all ways!

Across the road from Beamhurst Hall was a big farm kept by Mr and Mrs Frank Bailey. Every Thursday I had to take a clean, empty bottle with a cork in it. When I called on Saturday it would be filled ready for me – with top of the churn cream. What a gift it was in those days. It would whip up to go on a trifle or with fruit, or just the job for tea or coffee; grand stuff. Yet these kindly people suffered such ill luck. Mrs Bailey lost her youngest daughter with polio. 'Polio', or infantile paralysis, was a scourge of the fifties and several of my customers lost children with this disease. Mrs Bailey always maintained that it had come on the paper of a letter – she'd had a letter from someone in Germany, where the disease was most prevalent. Mrs Bailey's husband also died when quite young.

Before I relate the following story let me say that I do not believe in superstition or luck in any shape or form! As I arrived in Bailey's yard one Saturday afternoon, Mr Bailey (Frank's father) also arrived in his car. He got out, and had with him a small basket of parsley plants. To me this was a strange sight, as superstition abounds around parsley, and people say that to transplant it brings death. He could obviously see my surprise and asked why. I told him and he laughed! When I went there again on Monday, Mrs Bailey said: "Have you heard our sad news, John?" I said "No". She said, "Frank's father passed away suddenly during the weekend."

I now left the hamlet of Beamhurst, turning into the very narrow Watery Lane. Carefully round the first corner of the lane as there was a spring here which ran into a stone trough and the local women would often be here fetching water in buckets. There was a ford across the road here as well.

Old Mrs Brookes kept a small farm at the side of the road where she lived with her unmarried daughter, Edie. Mrs Brookes was in the same class as my Grandma when they were at Hollington School. She would often say: "How's Lizzie?" Mrs Brookes had been a widow for thirty years and had a hard life bringing up her family. Granny Walker, the old midwife at Stramshall, once told me that Mrs Brookes had both her husband and small daughter dead in the house at the same time, in the influenza epidemic at the end of the First World War.

My next call on the left was a widow in similar circumstances. Mrs Mellor at Park Cottage had one son and four daughters. Her husband had been killed at Fauld, when the ammunition dump exploded there in 1944. This was the biggest 'man-made' explosion of all time when it happened, although even this was superseded by the atomic bomb the following year. Albert Mellor had to walk about threequarters of a mile to catch the special works bus, which picked him up at Stramshall Church. On the morning of the fateful explosion, Albert had been late getting up which was most unusual, and his wife said: "You will never catch the bus, Albert, you will have to stop at home today." He decided that he would just about make it in time. Unfortunately he did – and was killed in the explosion at midday.

Mr Richardson lived at the Flashes Farm with his housekeeper, Bertha Ward, an adopted daughter, Annie, and her husband Ernie. Old Mr Richardson was a very thin man with a small grey beard who always wore a milking slop. He used to say: "Hard work never killed anybody. It's too much of it that kills you!" These people were all getting on in years. When old Mr Richardson and Bertha died, Annie and Ernie sold up and retired to a new house which they had built for themselves. They suffered ill health for years, yet incredibly, both lived to be in their eighties! They both loved to get hold of a bit of 'news' and couldn't wait for me to arrive to share it. Annie would say: "Let me tell him, Ernie!"

And now on to New House Farm. This was the last farm before entering the village of Stramshall. Mrs Arthur Pattinson lived here. She was an excellent cook and baker. Her short pastry was really good, in fact she was the best paste maker I ever knew – she had that essential knack for making paste.

CHAPTER SEVENTEEN
More characters from the Stramshall area

The houses in Stramshall were quite close together and I would supply about ten houses before moving my van on to do a similar number. I would sometimes have my hair cut at Mrs Bostock's. Old Jack, her husband, was a retired railwayman and he would use a green railway signalling flag to put around my neck to catch the falling hair! These were council houses and a Mrs Peach also lived here. When someone in the district died, she and her friend Mrs Lowe, would set off on foot, often during the night, to do the essential job of 'laying out'. This necessary but often unpleasant task meant undressing the body and washing and drying it. The body was then put on a flat board and the arms and legs straightened out before the body became cold and 'set'.

One might imagine these two people to be morbid, straight-laced and perhaps even fearsome! Not a bit of it, they were the happiest and kindest people you could ever wish to meet, always laughing and finding a bit of fun in their hard and difficult lives!

Next to Mrs Peach lived Mrs Avery. She had a picture on the wall of her living room which showed her son Harry and myself leading a Company of soldier cadets through Uttoxeter during the war. Harry was a Company Sergeant Major and I was either a Sergeant or a Corporal, I can't remember which.

Tom Dawson was a specialist in farm work, a country craftsman. His services were always in demand by local farmers and his finished work was a joy to see. He was an expert at 'laying hedges'. On this job he was continually sharpening his axe and hook and was never satisfied with them unless they would shave the hair off the back of his hand! Any saplings, such as oak, ash or holly, would be left standing. All 'rubbish' and unwanted growth of elder, blackberry and nightshade would be cleared out of the hedge bottom. Tom of course also did ditching and all types of fencing such as post and rail, and he tightened wire fences where necessary.

Mrs and Mrs Plant were an old retired couple. He did all the housework – he would always have a duster in his hands – because his wife was so badly crippled with rheumatism. At bedtime he would get a flat piece of wood and put it under one foot at a time and lift each foot from one stairs tread to the next to enable his wife to get upstairs. This couple were excellent wine makers and they taught me a lot about making wine. Most people at this time made wine and were proud of their prowess at it, just as they were with their jams, chutneys, pickles and other preserves. Perhaps damson wine was the most widely made wine, and of course elderberry, which obviously used the plentiful fruits of the neighbourhood. In the same way, on poor ground, where birch trees abounded, birch wine was the order of the day. Birch wine contains no water; it is made entirely from the sap of the birch tree. The trees are tapped in early March and cold, windy weather is best. A hole is bored about twelve inches up from the ground – no need for it to go in more than ¾" to 1" as the sap runs just under the bark layer. The hole can be ¼" or ⅜" and a small piece of rubber tubing is inserted to let the sap run clear of the tree and into a jar. I use a toffee jar. Some people just put a piece of rag in the hole and into the jar. In twenty four hours the jar will probably be full of sap, perfectly clear and just like water. This sap should be used the same day, as it does not keep wholesome longer than one day.

I will give the recipe in case anyone should wish to try this very good but very potent wine!

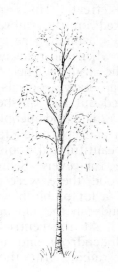

BIRCH WINE
1 gallon of sap,
3lb sugar
½ ounce of yeast
1 orange and 1 lemon

Boil the sap and sugar for an hour, skimming now and again. Pour into a tub containing the juice and thinly pared rinds of the fruit. Leave to cool; when just tepid, stir in the yeast. Cover well and leave for four days. Skim well, then strain into a clean dry cask that it will fill. Do not cork it or fasten it down.

Leave it to ferment, but keep covered at all times to keep out wine flies. It will have finished working in about a month; bubbles will have stopped coming up. Cork down and leave for three months. Then carefully siphon the wine from the lees into bottles, cork down and leave to mature for another few months.

Sap can also be gathered from walnut and sycamore trees and used in the same way.

Now and again, over the years, other bread suppliers would try to create a bread round for themselves. At one time a firm even came from about twenty miles away, hawking bread around the Stramshall area every day – as opposed to my three times a week. They only did this for a while and then finished. I knew it was not a commercially viable operation, calling with bread every day. They even went so far as to tell some of my customers that they would run me off the road!

The family of Mellors lived on a hilltop farm at Stramshall. They belonged to an old and prolific family of local craftsmen. Old Tom who lived here with his wife Selina was the last of these craftsmen who were joiners, wheelwrights, builders and undertakers. Old Tom had a very high pitched voice, as if it had never broken. He made coffins, which were always slightly turned out on each side at the foot end, giving a 'fish tail' effect. His grandparents worked on the railway crossing houses around here, which were built when the railways were laid

Fish tail coffin.

in the 1840s. Their woodwork can still be seen – the heavy timber barge boards were usually painted white, looped and fretted out and finished off with a strong white finial spike.

The old people's unmarried son and daughter survived them and continued farming here, while the joiner's shop with all its beautiful old tools gradually fell into disrepair and has now gone for ever. Selina once told me that "when we lived at Bigwood there were a lot of birch trees there. Way used fert mak' a lot of birch vine. Way bored holes in the trays wi' a nail bit and ran the sap out of 'em wi' a goose fither!"

At the centre of Stramshall village there is an island of rhododendrons and a single large oak tree. Fenced off well with iron railings (in those days), this small area is known grandly as the 'Park'! Leaving the van here I would deliver to the dozen or so houses nearby, on foot. One dark winter's evening it was pouring with rain as I returned to my van to refill my basket and I found that I couldn't open the back doors on the van. The doors were opened with a square carriage key, which I carried in my coat pocket. After a lot of fiddling about, I discovered that the hole was blocked inside. After a lot of time wasting and effort I removed the blockage. It was an acorn. Some boys hat put it there and were having a good laugh somewhere at my expense!

I would generally walk up to the vicarage from here, as most incumbents did not take kindly to a bread van being driven over the gravelled forecourt in front of the vicarage! One of the Vicars here was the Reverend Beck. He got on well with the parishoners, as they did with him. At least that was so until the Queen's Coronation in 1953. Stramshall, like all towns and villages, had a huge tea party in the village hall. I think Granny Walker cut the big iced Coronation cake I had made and Mrs Plumpton gave out the Coronation mugs. Mrs Plumpton was in her nineties and the oldest inhabitant. She was born in Stramshall and had taught at the village school there. At this time television was not in general use, although there was the odd set here and there. The vicar had a set and made it known that he would be watching the Coronation on this television set and would not be at the party. I am afraid this was the beginning of the end for the Reverend Beck. The parishoners boycotted him and he was eventually moved to a living in Cheshire.

I once had an order for him, an order for cakes for a Sunday School party. It was on Christmas eve. Before I left the bakehouse, these cakes were all put up on a board and I pushed it on the cake board runners in the van, pushing it to the front, out of the way and more importantly, out of sight! During the day whilst delivering, I suppose more owing to the effects of drink than anything else, this board of cakes had come forward and they had got mixed with and been used along with the other buns and cakes which I had on for sale!

Completely forgetting about the order, I had got as far as the vicarage drive, when the Reverend Beck appears in a bit of a fluster! "Oh, John, it's two o'clock and we are ready for the cakes. Can I take them up with me now?" Well, I had hardly anything left, mainly eccles cakes and sugar buns and a few pieces of college cake! I apologised and put everything I had on a board for him and told him kow lucky he was! He was quite pleasant about it and very kindly never mentioned it again!

Stramshall Chapel

Chapel House was next to Stramshall Chapel. Mr and Mrs Jim Bott lived there. Jim was a roadman who retired early after a very serious heart attack. It was his wife's job to keep the Chapel clean – this work was tied to the tenancy of the cottage. Jim's favourite story, or should I say epic, was about the time he was a youth and was ploughing at Ellastone with a pair of horses and ploughed up a hornets' nest. This was re-lived in every detail, how the hornets got after him and the horses, the horses going through hedges before finally parting company with the plough, their harnesses and the hornets! Old Jim must have lived for another thirty years, having several more heart attacks and strokes. He still managed to come out on top. I saw him many times walking into Uttoxeter market with a zimmer frame! You couldn't keep old Jim down!

Next to the Chapel House was the Hollies where Mr and Mrs Fred Foulkes lived. It was a nice house, built at the turn of the century by a Mr Woodward, long since dead. His several properties at Stramshall had passed on to his daughter, Miss Adelaide Woodward, who lived at Uttoxeter. I would often meet Miss Woodward collecting her rents at Stramshall. She owned the Hollies, a cottage near it belonging to Mrs and Mrs Gotheridge, and also Mrs Lowe's Church Farm. If it was raining she would have an umbrella which was torn and mended with sticking plasters. Her wellington boots were also repaired in the same manner.

Mrs Lowe's would be her last call and Mrs Lowe would give her a cup of tea. Here, Miss Woodward would tip her money out onto the table and count it all. Then she would turn all the coins over so that they were all heads up and count it again. Then it would all be deftly turned over again, all tails up and recounted before going into paper bags and put in her pocket. Why she did this I have no idea. How we used to laugh about it all!

A small cottage next to the Hollies, which has now disappeared, was the home of Mr and Mrs Gotheridge and their daughter Connie. Poor Connie was mentally retarded but was just about safe enough and capable enough to live at home with her parents. She could not read or write or use money, but could do household chores. Understanding what she said was always a problem, often leading to her annoyance and a display of temper. In their small living room, Connie once picked up the carving knife and came for me – but a sharp word from her father soon quietened her down again.

Mr Gotheridge, whose Christian name was Eustace, was always called 'Yewdy'. As a youth he came to Stramshall from Swadlincote when the Chapel was built. He was a bricklayer all his life. Mrs Gotheridge, whose name was Agatha, 'Aggie', was a big woman, tall and stout and always dressed in black. She was like a local 'newsagency' from which all the local news, gossip and rumour was distributed to all she met. This news was generally given while she wagged her finger and rolled her eyes, saying:

"Now dunna yow tell anyone I've towd y'!" She was a native of Stramshall, with her sister Fanny, the daughters of Mr and Mrs Harvey who sold fish and lived in a house opposite to Trafalgar House. There is only a stable building there now at the roadside. Aggie and Fanny were both excellent wine makers; in fact I had a wine barrel off each of them.

Yewdy was a man of upright and straightforward character. He once told me this story: "When I was a youth, a bricklayer, at Swadlincote, I used to have piles. I had them so bad that I would have to sit on the shaft of my brick hammer to push them back." (I should think this would be more painful than even the piles!) "Once I was off work with them and a gypsy came to the door and asked me what was the matter. I told her I'd got piles and she said that she'd tell me how to cure them. 'When you are going about you will sometimes see an old boot, perhaps in the hedge bottom or somewhere, one with plenty of hobnails in it. Take the boot and put it on a really good fire. When it is glowing red hot, drop it in a bucket of water. Pull your trousers down and carefully lower yourself over the steam. Keep doing it as much as you can bear it.'" Yewdy said he did this and never suffered from piles again all his life!

I had piles myself and kept a sharp lookout for a suitable old boot. It must have been a couple of years before I eventually spotted one. It was in some old rubbish along Watery Lane. Well, I tried old Yewdy's remedy, but it was no use to me – I had to have an operation in 1960!

Yewdy liked his cakes and bread burnt black! Sometimes Aggie would make pancakes, occasionally about the time I arrived there around five o'clock. She would say: "Dun yow want a pace of ponceek, John?" Her pancakes were not the thin ones we call pancakes, but were about an inch thick, which she would cut into portions. One piece was usually sufficient! I well remember one Thursday night, she poured me out a cup of tea which proved to be very hot and strong. Instead of being open and asking for more milk, I waited until Mrs Gotheridge turned and went into the back kitchen. Then, keeping one eye on the door, I reached out quickly for the milk jug, misjudged its position and pushed it over! What a mess! I had a bit of explaining to do then and it served me right! At least it was not quite as bad as the situation my Dad once found himself in! Someone gave him a glass of home made stout – quite undrinkable, he said – and standing at the back door, while the person had gone to fetch her purse, my Dad turned and threw the stout out of the glass towards the backyard fence. Only then did he notice a carpet had been spread out across the fence – too late – the carpet was decorated with a broad black stripe!

Anyway, to return to Mrs Gotheridge, what a grand old character, she was nearly always to be seen in the road by her house, walking with her swaying gait and waiting either to give some news or to receive it. She didn't believe in using one word when two or three would do instead! The old couple must have been worried about what would happen to Connie after they had both passed away. Yet when the time came, owing to the kindness of neighbours and friends, Connie managed all right. They handled money for her, paying for her coal and bread and made sure she was always clean and tidy.

Part of the Hare and Hounds pub was a cobbler's shop kept by Mr Tom Griffin. He made boots and shoes as well as mending them, just as my two uncles did at Rocester. Old Tom was stone deaf and had an eye which was not straight. He was such a pleasant old fellow; his face lit up and beamed whenever he met you. His wife was just the same, always so happy. They had quite a big family, most of them living locally, but were all afflicted in some way with eye and ear trouble.

Old Tom had two sisters living next to the pub. Annie was born deaf and dumb but her sister, Mrs Mycock, was all right. Annie was younger than her sister and did most of the housework. One Saturday, Annie was on her knees whitening the step when Mrs Mycock her sister came behind her to say something and touched Annie on the back, as she was deaf. Annie thought that her sister had pushed her and a fight ensued. Annie threw the step rag in Mrs Mycock's face, whitening her glasses, and then fled in panic to the Hare and Hounds! This was of course an exceptional incident in the lives of these normally very quiet and gentle people.

Dairyhouse Farm was the home of Mr and Mrs Joe Hollins. Joe was very lame in one leg. He delivered milk with a horse and float and he had difficulty getting in and out of the

Stramshall: Hare and Hounds and Chapel

float, but he seemed to have got used to it. Mrs Hollins was stone deaf. On one occasion when Don called with the bread, he walked in as usual and Mrs Hollins was undressed, ready for the bath. She did not see or hear Don go in, so he left the bread and very quickly departed! I have since thought that when she saw the bread on the table it may have been a bigger shock than to have actually seen Don come in!

Long since gone is the wheelwright and joiner's shop of Charlie Ede, next to Dairyhouse Farm. He was an undertaker and a very fine craftsman. During the war he made several inventions. These patterns were made in wood and sent to the Ministry of Defence. I remember one invention was for an interlocking track to be used on tanks and armoured vehicles. It made the changing or repair of damaged tracks so much easier and quicker.

Charlie was a friend of my Dad's and they would go shooting together. I often went with them and once went for a few days shooting in Wales. Charlie's place had a very big garden and it was owned by Mr Tom Griffin. One of Charlie's hobbies was the growing of fruit trees. He would grow the young stocks and then graft onto them his fruiting wood or 'pens' as he called them. Charlie was very skilled at grafting and had a pear tree growing on a hawthorn stock. His huge and luscious Victoria plums were without equal in this district. They were trained on the sides of his sheds and also free standing aroung his big garden. Not only the plums but the leaves were so much bigger than those we have today. He also always kept a few pigs and my Dad would kill and dress them for him.

At the back of his buildings, on some spare ground, was a big concrete circle with a depression in the centre. This was used for fitting the iron tyre onto the wooden wheels which Charlie made for his carts. The wheel would be assembled and laid on this concrete circle with the hub in the centre hole, and nearby a fire would be made. The iron tyre, made slightly smaller than the wooden wheel, would be heated in the fire to expand it, then it was carried with tongs by Charlie and his assistants and quickly dropped in place over the wooden wheel. It would now be dowsed with water, causing it to shrink on tightly to the wooden wheel. Village people would often come and congregate here to watch this job! Poor Charlie died of a very sudden heart attack still in his early fifties.

Coming to the. end of the Stramshall round, I now crossed over into Broomy Close Lane. There were not many houses along here then, but a lot more council houses were built in the fifties. My last call was at Mr William Walker's. He was a Methodist preacher and with his wife kept a small farmstead where he milked a couple of cows and kept a few hens. There was a nice warm 'early' garden here and in the south facing border under the house window, he always had a nice show of the early tulips, Kaiser Kroon.

Each year at Stramshall Horticultural Show I was called upon to judge entries in the cake classes, also in the classes for eggs, jam, pickles and other homemade preserves. Usually in the cake class I would provide a 'set' recipe for the cake, varying it each year – fruit cake, madeira, jam sponge cake, for instance.

On Bank Holiday Mondays we always worked, but finished early, about three o'clock in the afternoon! If we did not work on these days, it meant that all the Monday rounds had to be done on Tuesday as well as the Tuesday rounds. There was also the bakehouse work on Tuesday, preparing for the Wednesday market day and it was just not feasible to have Monday as a holiday. Anyway, it fitted in with one of my Grandma's favourite reminders to me: "The devil makes work for idle fingers." Aren't those few words so true?

When the Alton Towers leisure park was opened, Bank Holiday traffic was a great problem. Sometimes traffic would be at a standstill from Alton way back for eight miles to Uttoxeter, even as late as 1.30pm. I wonder that some of them even got into the Park that same day!

CHAPTER EIGHTEEN
Rocester

Every Friday morning we did a bread and cake round in Rocester village. Starting at Churnet bridge we worked our way through the village, to be at the 'Mill' for twelve o'clock. At this time everyone turned out of the Mill for their dinner hour, and it was a very hectic time supplying the women with the goods they wanted, knowing that they were all in a hurry to get home!

Arkwright's Cotton Mill was the major employer of labour in the Rocester area until the advent of the JCB factory. The mill is now closed down and the building is in fact now owned by the JCB factory.

Don always did this Rocester round. I only did it during the two weeks of the year when Don would be on holiday. My Grandma's was one of the last calls in Rocester – she lived in the last house of a terrace of twenty four houses. We had a cup of tea here and always made sure we had saved her 'usual' order, a small tin loaf and a bun loaf, also a couple each of buns, custards and small cakes. This would last her until Wednesday's market when she would have another small tin loaf.

This was a 'dead end' and we had to turn the van round here, in quite a restricted space. Every two houses had a shared back yard, most of the yard space taken up by a big water tub, one at each house. My Grandma's was a 72 gallon wooden barrel standing on bricks and always covered with a wooden lid – amongst other things to keep the light out which would turn the water a green cast. One day a vehicle was trying to turn round, using every available inch of space, when it hit Grandma's water tub. The owners of the vehicle replaced it after some time but this was not the major concern of Grandma. Although she had water 'on tap', this was only used for cleaning and cooking. Rainwater was always used for washing and bathing. This lovely soft water was without equal and Grandma soon pronounced her verdict on washing with tap water. "It's that hard it fair makes your fingers whistle!"

Despite the reasonable prosperity of Rocester, sanitation had not advanced a great deal. Older houses and farms still had earth closets, generally built down the garden and enhanced with a

COTTON MILL, ROCESTER.

Cotton Mill, Rocester

High Street, Rocester

lilac bush or an elder tree. The contents would be dug out annually, in Spring, and tipped into a trench in the garden. This would be the site of the kidney bean row. Other uses for this free fertiliser were often tried. An old fellow at Stanton tried it under his celery. He said he had the best celery "he ever growed" – huge white sticks. On enquiring about the flavour, his tone altered and his voice dropped, "Way cudne ate it – yew cud taste the muck in it – I dug it ow up and sowd it ow in Derby market." Oh well! What the eye never sees, the heart never grieves!

Most of the later 'mill' houses had a lavatory with a galvanised iron bucket which was emptied by a man who came once a week. This type of lavatory was often referred to as the 'janker'. The army slang for punishment was derived from this word. Going 'on jankers' originally meant emptying these buckets in barracks and camps as a type of punishment.

The man who emptied these buckets in Rocester came with a horse and a high-sided cart which was known as 'the Brandy Wagon'. He was called variously the mixen man, miskin man or by the more down-to-earth name of the muck man! This collection always took place on Friday – our day for delivering bread and cake in the village! The women slammed their doors shut, to help keep out the smell as the miskin man emptied the buckets into his cart. Often the buckets would be very full and he would inevitably spill some on the ground. He would then immediately get the sharp edge of the womens' tongues, shouting from within the house! We had to race down to the houses before he reached them, and then return to those he had been to – after a decent interval!

My Grandma lived at number 24, the last house, and after a cup of tea there, we left Rocester. The miskin man also finished there; his cart was full and it was time for his dinner break. The horse would be told to 'stand', the full cart leaking at the corners where the 'brandy' ran from it in thin streams. The man would then sit down on some grassy clods with his back to the fence, take his cap off and wipe his hands on it, before getting his lunch bag out and enjoying his sandwiches!

Some houses would be so overrun with mice that the householders kept their groceries in baskets which hung from hooks on the ceiling beams.

High Street, Rocester

Friday didn't seem to be an ideal day for taking bread and cakes round! Pedley's bone wagon also called at the butchers' shops in Rocester on Friday mornings. This open wagon collected all the unwanted waste meat, skins, offal, feet and hides. These were all carried out and and thrown onto the ever-growing collection from other shops and villages. The smell was atrocious, and made the brandy wagon seem like a flower shop by comparison.

I used to go to Rocester with Don every Friday but after getting into the village I would go and call on a few of my old relatives who lived there. First of all I would go to the 'Boot Shop' and see my Uncle Joe and my Uncle Amos who would be mending shoes in the 'back shop'. Uncle Amos's crippled daughter also lived here with them. She was struck with paralysis at the age of eleven whilst living as a boarder at Leek High School. Grace had apparently got out of bed in the night for a drink of water and was struck down and spent the rest of her life in a wheelchair. She was a most happy and pleasant person, always laughing and yet so incapacitated. She had leg irons and it took her four hours to get up and get dressed each morning.

Uncle Joe and Uncle Amos were my Grandad's younger brothers. Joe was born in 1870 and Amos in 1867. These old men could not only repair boots and shoes, but could also make them, just as did their father, Joseph Forrester, my Great Grandad. What a pity this old workshop with all its tools and other equipment was allowed to disappear. It was a museum in itself – completely unaltered and just as it was a century before. Great Grandad's empty seat was still there. On the whitewashed brick walls were religious scripts in frames and other Victorian admonitions such as "Cleanliness is next to godliness." There were cricketing invitations (Uncle Joe was a wicket keeper and played in his last match when he was 70!) and of course, rows of tools inserted in lines of leather loops. On one wall there were a lot of pairs of wooden shapes around which boots and shoes were made. These were called 'lasts' and each pair would be for a particular person. There were one or two odd lasts and Uncle Joe said these were for men with a wooden leg. I didn't know whether he was joking or not!

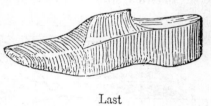

Last

Looking down on the scene was a picture of Great Grandad, white fuzzy beard and sidewhiskers with a clay pipe and a black beret on his head. He was still loved and venerated by these old men, who were his children. The little iron stove which provided warmth was kept going with discarded leather soles and heals which had been removed for repairs. All the rainwater from the workshop roof ran into a huge stone cistern in the back yard where sides of leather would be kept soaking. There was even a length of gutter which ran on the inside of the workshop wall. This carried water from the furthest roof to the cistern. Why it was not on the outside of the building I don't know, but it entered at one end, ran the length of the workshop – about nine feet up the wall – through a hole over the window and across the yard into the cistern! The problem of draughts evidently was never considered!

Uncle Amos died first. He was well in his eighties, but Uncle Joe kept working until he was ninety. To watch this old craftsman work was an education in itself. You may think that the strong cobbler's thread, used for sewing on the leather soles, was bought on reels! No such thing – it was made! Uncle Joe would pull a handful of white stuff out of a cupboard by his seat, it was just like cotton wool. Using both hands he would deftly twist and roll it a few times on his apron, pulling it at the same time, and it would become a long white thread. Russian hemp he said it was. This thread was now passed tound a small nail in a bench about two feet away, keeping it tight. This double thread was then waxed together by drawing a piece of cobbler's wax along it a few times. This thread was now strong enough to hold a horse. A bristle about 2½ inches long was attached to each end of this thread, these were Russian boar's bristles – Uncle Joe said all other bristles split at the ends, but these did not.

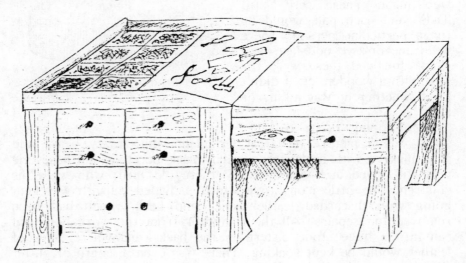

The Cobbler's Stool

The black thread or 'tachin end' as they called it was now ready for use. The new leather sole would be lightly fixed in place and holes pierced through it with a sharp awl which would coincide with the holes in the shoes 'upper' from which the old thread had been removed. One end of the thread, or rather the bristle, would be pushed up through the first hole and the other end likewise. This bristle would be pushed down through the same hole and drawn as tight as sewing progressed. When the job was finished he would get three small brass sprigs about ⅜" long – tingles he called them. These would be driven in the sole where it met the instep, always in a triangular pattern – this was Uncle Joe's mark. Uncle Amos's mark was two tingles in side by side. Uncle Joe said he once saw a pair of shoes he had mended in Skegness!

Every Friday as we had a cup of Camp coffee together, he would tell me some interesting facet of his life or of his family or perhaps of the local history. Although of course young people do not as a rule pay much attention to such tales, fortunately I could remember most of them in detail and they gave me a most interesting insight into life in the reign of Queen Victoria.

Uncle Joe said one day that his mother and father, my great grandmother and great grandfather, remembered Queen Victoria's accession to the throne in 1837. His father was born in the reign of King William IV and his mother, who was four years older, was born in the reign of King George IV.

So before leaving the Boot Shop, let me recall one or two stories he told me. Uncle Joe's father and mother had nine children, eight boys and one girl. Every dinner-time during the summer they had rhubarb, either in a pie, stewed or in a boiled pudding. This was from May to September and the pudding was always eaten first. In this way they could fill up on the cheaper part of the meal. Meat, which was expensive, would be the second part of the meal and was boiled in a big pot on the fire and the vegetables cooked with it. The potatoes which didn't require so long were put in a net and dropped in later! From the youngest child to the eldest was a span of thirty years. His mother was also a midwife for the village and the local district. Gosh, she must have been busy!

He said that in August 1912, his parents had been married for 60 years, their diamond wedding. Of course in those days nobody had any money, there was no fancy cake or expensive presents; just a few friends and neighbours would go in and have a cup of tea with them. Only their own children or close relatives would buy a bit of something. Uncle Joe said that he bought his Dad two or three bottles of beer and his Mother a few handkerchiefs. He said it was on a Saturday and it was bitterly cold although it was August, and, as he always went to Uttoxeter on Saturdays, he decided to call on the old people first. It was before eight o'clock in the morning and they had got a roaring fire and were so pleased to see him.

One of their grandchildren, Annie, visited later in the day and she described the scene to me like this: "Grandma and Grandad were retired from the Boot Shop and lived at 42 High Street, Rocester. There was only a living room and a kitchen and you walked straight into the living room off the pavement. I walked in and they never saw me or heard me. They were kneeling down on the rug in front of the fire, holding hands and saying their prayers. Grandad had got a couple of bottles of beer sticking up in each jacket pocket. I quietly backed out and closed the door. They had been married 60 years that day."

Uncle Joe said that, in the late 1800s, tobacco firms decided to try and find out who were their biggest users of tobacco. Shops were asked to take note of their best customers and how much they smoked. He said that in the whole of Staffordshire the contest had been narrowed down to two men; his Dad and Mr Twemlow who was the surveyor of Leek. He said that his Dad smoked two ounces of light shag a day and Mr Twemlow came second at one and a half ounces a day!

Uncle Joe himself was certainly the biggest user of tobacco that I knew. He smoked a pipe, cigarettes and took snuff! He said that when Woodbines first appeared you could buy five Woodbines and one match for a penny!

From the Boot Shop, I would walk on a bit and call on Bert and Polly. They had retired from the painting and decorating business. Bert was my mother's cousin. Polly, the poor old soul, was blind and deaf in her old age – as she said, just like her mother had been before her. They both loved a pinch of snuff. The taking of snuff was always a big concern at Rocester – with it being a mill town, smoking at work was not allowed, so of course snuff assumed the major role as tranquilliser! The few shops in Rocester not only sold snuff in tin boxes but also loose, when it was weighed out into a small paper bag. Some customers would take their own snuff boxes and the shopkeeper would fill them up, knowing from regular use exactly how much each box held.

After these calls on relatives, I would walk back home for my dinner, while Don finished his delivering in Rocester. After, he would call for me at Station Road where I lived, and we would start out and deliver to houses once again.

About a hundred yards from my house lived an interesting and upright old lady by the name of Mrs Elsie Pattinson. Her husband Bill, who was a mason, worked at the local stoneyard of Stanton and Bettanys. Known then affectionately as Mrs Pat, her late father and her brother were both Registrars of Births, Marriages and Deaths at Rugeley. Mrs Pat had been married before, to Jack Tortoishell and she was known then as Mrs Tot! Jack had been a First War soldier and they lived on a smallholding at Denstone. Jack returned from the war a sick man, wounded and gassed and his great friend, one of the Bleything brothers from Quixhill, was in a similar poor way. He soon died and Jack went to his funeral. In the Denstone churchyard, Jack turned to his wife and said, "I shall be the next one in here, Elsie." And he was. Mrs Tot was left in poor circumstances and with a crippled daughter to add to her troubles. Even so, by sheer hard work, she coped, and also managed to look after her own parents and brother and sister in their last days.

Mrs Tot was fortunate in those days in having a part time job, helping Mrs Wrottesley at Denstone Vicarage. But this was no easy job and she nearly lost it when Mrs Wrottesley discovered that she would often call at the Tavern for a glass of Guinness! But Mrs Tot was as good as a nurse to Mrs Wrottesley and dressed and bandaged her bad legs for her every day – she said the smell was awful. Monday morning was 'wash day,' and Mrs Tot said, "One Monday, I was busy doing the washing and I saw Mrs Wrottesley coming across the field. I knew what the old bitch was coming for. She knocked and walked in. It was the custom to immediately offer a chair and a cup of tea, but I just carried on with my work, after saying: 'Good morning, Mrs Wrottesley.' Then she opened up: 'I saw your daughter in the village a couple of days ago and she did not curtsy to me.' I stood straight up, faced her and looked her straight in the eyes. 'Mrs Wrottesley, it says in the Bible that at the name of Jesus every knee shall bow. If I ever see my daughter curtsy to you, I will cut the legs from under her. Now I am a very busy woman and have got a lot of work to do, so I will bid you good day.'"

Just before Mrs Wrottesley died, she said to Mrs Tot:

"Elsie, when I have died I want you to burn two candles in the room until I am buried, and if you don't, I shall come back and haunt you." Mrs Tot replied: "Yes, I will certainly burn the candles for you, but as regards you coming back and haunting me, I'm not frightened of that at all!"

Mrs Tot had a Christian faith which was as strong as the Rock of Gibraltar. She was nursing a woman who was dying at Oak Farm; I can't remember the woman's name: "She was lying back in bed exhausted, all her pain seemed to have gone as her life slowly ebbed away. I sat with her waiting for the end. All of a sudden, Jack, she sat bolt upright, her face lit up in a smile and she streched both hands out in front of her and said: 'I'm coming – I'm coming.' Then she fell back unto the pillow again and passed away. She'd seen a vision, Jack, she'd seen something, there is no question about it. She'd seen and believed."

As I said before, Mrs Tot married again and her life was somewhat easier. She looked after her husband Bill in his last illness and lived on after his death until she was over ninety. Quite a character! But before leaving her let me tell you about her connection with Dr Palmer, the notorious murderer, who killed many people in Rugeley by poisoning them. When Mrs Tot was well in her eighties she said to me: "I had a grand night this week. My Grandson fetched me and I went to his house to watch a television programme on Dr Palmer. Oh, it was good, I did enjoy it!" She said her father knew Dr Palmer and walked from Yoxall, where they lived, to Stafford, about 12 miles, to see Dr Palmer hung at Stafford Gaol in 1856. When Mrs Tot was a girl she would go to Rugeley with her mother to visit an old lady there and this old lady, when she was a servant girl, worked for Dr Palmer and would often carry the poisoned porridge upstairs for the doctor's intended victim, unknown to her of course. She said the gruel often smelled so good that she would sneak a spoonful as she carried it up!

Dr Palmer had a medical practice in Rugeley and was well liked by the people; he often waived his fees for the poorest of his patients. His vice was gambling on horses and he soon got into debt. He insured his wife for £13,000, and soon afterwards she died and the Doctor benefited handsomely. The Doctor also had to pay out money towards an illegitimate son. This son died also, as did another patient who had begun to query the Doctor's ways. Well-bitten by the gambling bug, Dr Palmer bought a racehorse – not a very good one – and this put the Doctor in debt to a couple of men, who later also died! Dr Palmer at this point decided to insure his own brother for the same amount as he insured his late wife, £13,000. When this brother died, the insurance company refused to pay out the money.

Whilst attending race meetings, the Doctor had become very friendly with a man named John Cook, who also owned a racehorse and, better still, had just inherited £15,000. They went to Shrewsbury races together, to watch and gamble on their horses. Cook's horse, Polestar, won its race but the Doctor's horse, aptly named 'Chicken', was a loser. Cook and the Doctor both returned to Rugeley where Cook was lodging at a pub. The Doctor had no money left by now and Cook became ill. Despite all the careful medical attention that Dr Palmer gave to Cook and all the nourishing broths he made for him, Cook died!! His funeral was arranged by the doctor, despite protests from Cook's friends and relatives but then they discovered that Cook's money was missing. Dr Palmer was arrested and his trial took place at the Old Bailey where he was found guilty and sentenced to death.

Dr Palmer was one of the greatest experts in the world on poisons and despite post mortems and autopsies, the poison he used to kill his victoms was never discovered. He was hung in a gateway at Stafford Gaol in 1856, in order that as many people as possible could see him.

My Aunt Marjorie's father, Mr Tom Brown, who was a station master at Uttoxeter, lost two of his own cousins, poisoned by Dr Palmer. This infamous case made the people of Rugeley feel a dark shadow had been cast over their town and they petitioned Parliament to have the name of the town changed. It was amazingly proposed to them that the town be renamed after the Prime Minister, Lord Palmerston, and called Palmerstown! This was not accepted and in the end they decided to keep the name of Rugeley after all!

Whilst not wishing to continue at great length in a macabre vein, before closing this chapter let me tell you of the haunted house! The half timbered cottage was the scene of a suicide when a man living there cut his own throat. My Grandma remembered this happening, but would never say much about the event or anything else of like nature! She didn't think it right to feed my enquiring mind with gory details! Since the suicide took place, the cottage has been subject to strange noises and bumps and a cold wind would blow inside it now and again. One local man and his wife went to live there, even though most local people would not live there because of stories. But old Charlie was a real sceptic and the very last person to be put off by stories and tales. So he and his wife lived there and although they heard things for certain, it didn't bother these hardy people – until one night! Charlie went to bed first, leaving his wife downstairs. He hadn't been in bed long before he was lifted up a short distance off the bed and then let go to drop back again on the bed. This happened three times in quick succession. He then got up and went downstairs, white as a sheet. He told his wife about his ordeal. They slept downstairs from then onwards, until they eventually sold the place.

Charlie had an older brother, Albert, who lived next door to my Grandma for fifty years. Albert told me that as a young man he would earn an extra shilling or two by grave digging. He recalled that one grave he dug was for the suicide victim from this haunted cottage. "The grave was just inside the lytch gate, round the corner on the left. I had just about finished digging and was levelling the bottom of the grave with my shovel when I found a flat stone there. I thought it strange for the stone to be down there and cleaned it off and there were two flat stones butted up to each other, with a slight join between them. I got my crowbar and gave several good blows on the join. One of the stones broke at the edge where I hit it and the crowbar shot out of my hands. It went out of reach or sight. I just threw some earth in and covered the bottom of the grave, but I lost a good crowbar!!" I bet poor Albert would have been in need of some strong refreshment after that episode!

CHAPTER NINETEEN
The years of change

The 1950s and early 1960s saw an end to the large scale delivery of bread and the hawking of it from door to door. This period also saw the end of the majority of small bakehouses. Delivering was now no longer a viable proposition due to increased wages, vehicle expenses – dearer petrol and garage bills – and other overheads.

But also it was a fact that the more affluent society ate a great deal less bread and the new 'sliced bread' from the large manufacturers was hitting the big time. In 1954 we bought a shop at 111 Smithfield Road and cut out half of our bread rounds.

The shop at 111 Smithfield Road

Then in 1963 we bought the shop at 14 Cheadle Road and finished delivering bread, except for customers who had it with a grocery order, this of course making it a profitable transaction, and we retained the Friday morning bread and cake round in Rocester village, as this was a very 'compact' round.

The shop at 14 Cheadle Road

At this same period, the days of the horse drawn vehicle were just about finished. Bill Rushton, the greengrocer from Carter Street, was the last person in this district to use a horse and dray for deliveries. Bill took over the business from his uncle, also named Bill Rushton. Their stall was opposite to mine in the market and it was amusing to watch old Bill setting out his fruit and vegetable display on the stall. He would wear a cap and a bag apron around his waist, smoking his pipe all the time. He would pick out several nice red apples, spit on them, and then polish them up on his sleeve. These would be put in a prominent position in his display!

His nephew Bill seemed to finish his rounds about the same time as I did. How it made me appreciate the comfort of the van's cab. Poor Bill and his horse would often be seen going along, saturated in the pouring rain. Of course his fruit and vegetables were not damaged by the wind and rain – my bread and cakes were far too vulnerable! In the dark winter evenings he would have a couple of lamps on his dray, with their weak glimmers of yellow light. The wooden brake blocks which were tightened down on to the iron tyres of the back wheels had long since worn down. Now each one had an old boot sole nailed on to it, to provide a grip! The old brown and white horse always wore blinkers but he never got used to traffic or in fact any sudden movement or noise and would make a bolt if a piece of paper blew in front of him. When Bill took him to the market stall he was constantly taking fright and would object to anyone who tried to stroke him, except, of course, Bill.

I remember one very cold and frosty winter morning when young Bill arrived at his stall which, as I have said, was next to mine. He was pulling the heavily laden cart himself, in the shafts! It was all level road from his premises about 500 yards away. I said: "What's up, Bill?" He replied: "Oss inna very well, Jack. I went to the fayld to get 'im – I cud say ay wonna rate – I cudna find it in me 'art to bring him, so I left 'im theer." Yes, Bill thought a lot of him. The horse lived in a field by the cemetery house. Strangely enough, a few years later, again another very frosty winter's morning, Bill went for the horse and had a slight heart attack in the field. He never stood market or used the horse again. He continued to do a bit of greengrocery business from his shop but it was the beginning of the end for Bill. He had a wife who pre-deceased him but he had no family, thus bringing to an end a very old Uttoxeter family business.

The attachment men had for their horses was always evident. Jack Brassington was one of the council employees who erected stalls in the market. Jack had a horse-drawn dray with which he brought the wooden stall sections and poles into the market area. Jack's horse was much quieter than Bill's, despite the fact that his name was Ginger! Some years later, when tractors had taken over from horses, I said to Jack: "Whatever happened to Ginger?" He said that Ginger was at a farm, I can't remember where, but a few miles from Uttoxeter, and that he was well and happy. Jack said: "I goo and say him when I've got ayfe a dee off. I always like fert tak 'im a bit a summat – ee comes gallopin' up as soon as ee says may!"

Black and white horses were called 'piebald', brown and white 'skewbald' and brown horses with a black tail and mane 'bays'. My Grandad had a skewbald horse at Rocester. His name was Joe. Grandad never tied Joe up, as he did the other horses in the stables. Joe could walk about and look out over the open half door of the stables. Grandad would feed him about nine o'clock every morning, but some mornings he might be too busy getting bread out of the oven. When Joe thought it was time my Grandad was making an appearance, he would put his head over the half door and lift the latch with his chin! Then he would walk round to the bakehouse and look through the window. If my Grandad was at the oven he wouldn't be able to see Joe. Ezra Woodward and Jack Holmes who worked there would pretend not to see Joe at the window and carry on with their work. Joe would then go to the bakehouse door and give it a few smart taps with a hoof to let Grandad know that Joe needed his breakfast! These hard working, intelligent and faithful animals always endeared themselves to their owners. When Joe died my Granddad cried like a baby.

I well remember working at the bakehouse, very early one morning. I was on my own and working at the table in front of the window. I 'felt' that someone was watching me and I looked up to see a huge face and two big eyes staring at me through the window. It was Dick Hodgkinson's horse which had got out of its field; it gave me quite a shock! Old Dick lived at the top of our yard and had a couple of fields and some buildings. He kept pigs, a few cows and some hens. In summer I would hear him in his fields as early as 4.00am with his horse and mower clattering along. When old Dick's wife had died and his family left home, he would often bring bills and letters down to the bakehouse for us to read. He had never learnt to read or write. His voice was deeper than anyone else's I have ever known. He would talk about old Gregory being at the bakehouse in the last century and he could remember the sails of the windmill going round. He was a First World War veteran and would be in church on Armistice Day, holding his prayer book open in front of him like everyone else, although he could not read it. He was a skilled man at many jobs, from catching rabbits to mixing concrete. Dick's concrete never wore out; it was harder than iron because he

My Grandad on the left – the horse is Joe's predecessor
Taken at Rocester in the 1890s

used a lot of stones in it.

In his last years old Dick had breathing problems and would bring his big wooden armchair out and put it in the middle of the yard, by his front door, to help him to try and get his breath. A very heavy and robust fellow and quite bald – some people nicknamed him 'Bladder' which comes from the expression 'as bald as a bladder of lard'! (lard used to be sold in pigs' bladders) Old Dick was a real bit of bygone England. His father was a besom maker.

Kate lived near the bakehouse in a row of cottages called officially 'Bamford's Row' but locally known by all as 'Woppy's Nest'! Now and again old Kate would come down to the bakehouse and ask: "Please an y' got a small pace of dough, Master Walker, fert mak' a barmy dumpling?" She would then toddle off with her dough, a piece about as big as a teacup. The dough would be put in a warm place and left to swell up, then carefully lifted up and put in a big saucepan of boiling water for about twenty minutes. The dumpling would then be taken out and broken into the required number of portions with a couple of forks. It would not be cut as this would make it close and 'sad'. The dumpling would then be eaten with some treacle on it or with milk and sugar. The barmy dumpling makes not only a cheap meal but also a very tasty one!

When we finally stopped delivering bread in 1963, my customers told me how much I would miss going round with bread every day and they quite honestly wondered if I would be able to cope with the change. In fact I did indeed miss calling upon them all, with their wonderfully sustaining friendships. A great many continued to support me, by fetching their bread and cake from the shop and stall. Many of them, particularly older people, were unable to fetch their bread and in some cases their neighbours would collect bread for them.

All at once the continued success of the bakery business at the Heath was now entirely dependent on the successful operation of the shop at Cheadle Road. The other shop at Smithfield Road had been going for ten years and was worked by my Father and Don's wife, Betty. (Don and Betty lived on these shop premises for a few years until moving into their own house.)

The hours of opening at Cheadle Road were from 7.30am until 6.30pm, each and every day, except of course Sundays.

CHAPTER TWENTY
The new shop

I opened the shop on the first Monday with some trepidation and awaited my first customer. When she came in, I could not supply her. I have now forgotten what it was that she had asked for, but I did more or less sell everything except for this item apparently! This was a bad start. My next customer wanted a small bag of frozen peas and ten Gold Leaf cigarettes. These I was able to supply and I felt much easier from then onwards.

I never did a lot of shop work, mainly Saturday afternoons, dinner hours and other odd times. More time was now spent in the bakehouse. Don, Rhoda and myself were all getting older and although we were still able to do our work, it took us increasingly longer to do it! My Father always said: "You have got to love work in this job, liking work is not enough – you have really got to love it!"

In the seventies my son Paul came into the business from Fryer's Garage, where he had been working in the vehicle body shop. A few years later, in 1977, my eldest son John also started at the bakehouse. He had been on road and site construction work, operating a JCB digger. Another – yet another – saying of my Dad's was that "no-one is any good working for himself until he had worked for someone else; you don't know what life is until you have had your feet under someone else's table". At least we all seem to have complied with this criteria!

Paul left after some years to go as a representative for a ready mixed concrete firm. He now operates his own concrete business in Ashbourne. For some reason all my sons seen to have the inborn ability to get on well with all other people in the course of their business and careers; just as did my parents and grandparents.

More recently over the years, these small family bakery businesses have vanished from the scene of our native land. Luckily ours has been one of the rare survivors.

In April 1982 my son Peter was one of the first soldiers on the Falkland Islands, at the onset of the war there, when the Argentinians layed claim to the islands. He was there throughout the conflict and was awarded a Mention in Despatches. On his return I flew the Union Jack at the bakehouse. The flag still flies, as it did from the Windmill a century ago.

By now age and illness were taking their toll of such loyal workers as Don and Rhoda and other assistants had to be taken on. I found that I was no longer able to do as much work later in the day as I had been doing. Therefore, to cope with this slowing down process of my body, I needed to start earlier and finish earlier. I began work at 3.00am on the three busiest days. These were Wednesday, Friday and Saturday. On the 'easier' days of Monday, Tuesday and Thursday I started at 4.00am. This ensured that I would finish by five o'clock each day. Even so, just as my Father had said: "You can always find another job that needs to be done – you can work all night. You have got to pack up and leave it alone!"

Of course, getting up early entailed going to bed early. I invariably went to bed between 7.40 and 7.50pm. Nowadays these hours of work are known as 'unsocial hours', yet I knew an old man who lived in the nearby hamlet of Great Gate; he was a farmer and a joiner; all his working life he got up at 2.30am and went to bed at 7.30pm! This extraordinary old fellow lived into his nineties!

Before going to bed I would cut my sandwiches for the following day. These were always four good thick rounds of bread and butter, spread thinly with Marmite, the bread being very well baked – burnt black if possible. I would have a couple of these sandwiches and a cup of tea about 9.00am and another couple at dinner time, having a meal when I returned home. I found this routine was excellent and fitted in well with my job. Perhaps in some ways I may have been influenced in my eating habits by my Grandma, with all her quaint sayings and beliefs! Let me mention here a few. She would say: "You dig your grave with your teeth." She said that milk was not a good thing to drink, especially at night time – it gave you 'bad heads'. Contrary to modern thinking she used a lot of salt, not only sprinkled on her food, she also had a heap of it on the side of her plate, in which she dipped the tip of her knife and put it on each forkful of food! Grandma always maintained that you should always have a bite of something to eat with your first cup of tea each morning – a biscuit, a slice of bread or anything – otherwise it would 'gnaw your belly out all day'. I have always done this, my Father did likewise.

She was a great believer in Vaseline for everything – cuts, bruises, sores, aches and pains – always Vaseline! When Grandma left school, she worked in Hollington stone quarries making scythe stones, shaping the stones by rubbing one against another. Her Mother told her that, as a girl, Grandma was so weak and poorly looking that she didn't expect her to live to be eighteen years old. Her Mother thought she was 'consumptive' (tubercular). But as I have said, Grandma lived into her ninety-eighth year and never spent a night in hospital in her life!

In her later years she allowed herself the luxury of two teaspoons of whiskey in her first cup of tea each morning. As if one might view this as an extravagance she would often say: "I don't waste it you know, I only have two teaspoons, but of course if it runs over, I don't bother!"

CHAPTER TWENTY-ONE
The later years

Yes, the hard work of later years was of a different type to the hard work of earlier years, with all that hawking to be done each day, but, granted good health, hard work is a healing balm for the knocks of life. My Dad was a great believer in hard work for everyone, especially young people. He said that it kept your body fit and healthy and your mind active; you would then have neither the time, inclination or energy for doing wrong and getting into mischief. He always had an answer to any problem which appeared in one's journey through life and he believed in the Biblical admonition: "The man who will not work shall not eat."

In a similar vein, my Dad always warned of the dangers of greed, envy, coveting and the worship of money. These undesirable evils would be noticed and pointed out by him whenever they were seen and he would always illustrate his point with an apt phrase such as: "Money won't buy happiness, it only pays for illusions." Another saying of my Dad's was that "a millionaire can only eat and sleep and pay his way, he can't do any more than that and quite often he won't even be able to sleep."

It was not only my Father but also my customers who were quick to offer me the benefit of the their guidance whenever the occasion arose! Many years ago, in some very adverse weather, I said to a customer, (I think it was Annie Cope at Stramshall), "What bad weather!" She replied: "Eh, lad – there's no such thing as bad weather, there's all sorts of good weather. There are plenty of people lying in hospitals with arms and legs off, who would give anything to be standing where you are now – rain or no rain."

One day at Granny Walker's we both stood at the window and watched a bride dressed in white, leaving a nearby house for her wedding. Granny Walker started crying. I enquired what was wrong. She said that she always cried at weddings but never at funerals. She went on to say: "It's such a cold world today, with so much greed and selfishness in it. I wish that I could be in Heaven with th' door shut."

Yes, I think I could nearly fill a book with the wise

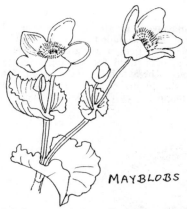

MAYBLOBS

country sayings I heard in abundance – and likewise the old country customs, long since gone, like the Mayblobs at Rocester. Every year on the first day of May, every home in the village of Rocester would put out a jar of water, containing a bunch of what we call locally 'Mayblobs'. The jar would be a glass jam jar in most cases. Mayblobs are the flowers known also as marsh marigolds or kingcups. These jars of flowers would be put outside the house by the door. Some would also be tied with string and suspended from a nail over the door and others on nails each side the door. The village scene looked grand with the brilliant enamel–like yellow of the Mayblobs and the green of their own leaves foiling them. This was beyond doubt a custom surviving from a pre-Christian era but alas, it disappeared with the upheavals of the 1939–45 war.

Another local custom, the making of frumety, continued for a few more years after the war ended but this now also seems to have long since faded away. Frumety was made from newly harvested wheat and was eaten mainly during the month of October at the time of the Rocester Wakes Fair. This fair, which still comes to Rocester, lasts for a week and is held during the week following the first Sunday after the ninth of October. The method of making frumety is as follows:

FRUMETY

The wheat is first of all washed in a bowl of cold running water, when any husk of chaff will float to the top and be washed away. The cleaned wheat is now put in a stew-jar and well covered with water, put in the oven and cooked slowly for eight hours or more, making sure it doesn't dry up. There is a special word for this slow cooking of the wheat, it is 'creeing' the wheat. The finished wheat will be nicely swollen and split open, very soft and will set quite firm in its own jelly when it is cold. Now to actually make the frumety, equal quantities of milk and water are brought to the boil and thickened with flour, as if making a thick white sauce. Sugar is added to taste and about three tablespoons of the creed wheat (if using a pint of milk liquor). Spice too is added, stir in half a teaspoon of pimento, also known as clove pepper or ground cloves. This particular spice is the only sort ever used for making frumety and gives it such a distinctive flavour. The whole is then cooked for a few minutes before serving. It should have the consistency of porridge and is eaten in a similar manner – with milk and sugar.

A bowl of frumety

Wakes cakes are also made, and in fact are still popular at this time of the year. These are not cakes as such but are large very rich short biscuits, about three inches in diameter. The making of these rich biscuits entails the use of nearly as much butter as flour. Baked only to a very pale colour, they are dredged over lightly with caster sugar on leaving the oven and when cool they are wrapped in greaseproof paper packets, six in each. There were eight or nine small bakehouses in Uttoxeter during the 40s and 50s and every autumn each one produced its own special Wakes cakes, made according to the proprietor's own 'secret recipe'! Certainly these seasonal goods were always much appreciated as a delightful treat when they appeared for a short while. Nowadays when one can buy mince pies in August and hot cross buns all the year round, the goods lose their appeal, just as each season perhaps loses its own excitement.

I suppose the making of frumety would have declined with the demise of the old cast-iron cooking ranges. These were used universally in this country for cooking and providing hot water. The constant source of heat was ideal for the creeing of the wheat. The iron ranges were installed mainly during the nineteenth century, even when the newer houses would have gas cookers. Before this time the local bakehouse would be used by people who brought along their own pies and bread to be baked for a small fee. There would also be a town or communal oven – in Uttoxeter this was situated at the rear of the Old Talbot and Town Hall (which was then in the Market Place).

With the advent of the ranges and more 'home baking' the public's use of the bakehouse ovens dwindled. Yet, still in keeping with tradition, the Sunday joint would often be taken to the nearest bakehouse. The joints were carried to the bakehouse in the people's own tins and put on the bakehouse table, payment being made there and then to the baker. According to the size of the tin it would be a penny or tuppence. Most joints would be of beef or mutton, but in winter pork would be the most popular choice of meat. Of course, pork was never eaten during the four months which had not got an 'r' in the name of the month! Many of the 'joints' would be rabbits, some of the larger and poorer families having a couple of rabbits to eat. All the roasted joints would be collected by their owners on return from church or chapel.

Some housewives would make a batter pudding and pour it around the joint to be roasted. Often on a Sunday morning, children would be given the task of delivering the joint to the bakehouse. This of course opened up the job to all sorts of hazards! They would play around and sometimes trip up and fall down, the meat and its tin flying in different directions, hastily retrieved and dumped back in the tin, well peppered with dust and gravel and devoid of all batter pudding if any had been used! The baker would take the tin of meat without question but, his all-seeing eye missed nothing. He would wash and clean up the meat and its tin. If batter had been in it he would get a spoon and skim a spoonful off all the other joints, give it a good stir up to obtain a uniform colour and pour it round the fallen joint! Thus, many a child never received the good hiding they expected on return from church! I wonder if they knew why? We did not do this Sunday baking and roasting. This was only done when the baker lived in or near the bakehouse – as did Jos Blore and John Gregory, our predecessors.

On Sunday afternoons these dinners were 'walked off'. Most people in small towns and villages would don their 'best clothes' and set out for a walk along the open roads and lanes.

There would be quite a lot of people on these walks, each family or group would stop and have a chat with others whom they met on the road.

With the beginning of the war in 1939, the meat roastings and the Sunday walks finished, but the Christmas roasting of meat and poultry continued until the 1970s. We did not work on Christmas Day, but the day before people would bring turkeys, geese, chickens and joints of meat to be roasted. These were all too large to go in the domestic ovens. Some people brought their birds in their own tins, others relied on us to provide a tin for them. I don't know if people ate these birds and joints cold on Christmas Day or what they did with them. Don and myself would be out delivering bread and Rhoda would be left in charge of this Christmas roasting. No charge was fixed for it but it was left to the discretion of the owner, who would give Rhoda half a crown or sometimes five shillings for herself. One man paid every other year! We noted with amusement that he passed away the year he was due to pay!

Some people put stuffing in their birds. A gypsy family came every year and they always made a very nice stuffing. It smelt grand and the aroma from it perfumed the oven and the bakehouse. Needless to say, I enquired how they made it but it was a 'secret'! As I said, even this Christmas roasting gradually phased itself out in the seventies, and in a way I was pleased to see it go. Not everyone came early. Some would even turn up at midday with big joints and birds to roast. Then there was the disposal of all the fat and grease and our tins to be washed and cleaned. During the roasting, fat would get onto the oven sole, producing a lot of acrid smoke until it had burnt itself away. It would be a couple of days before the oven had ridded itself of this infringement.

Many years ago some farmers had a custom of thrashing the grain out of the last sheaves of wheat to be harvested. Durose's farm at The Grange, Bramshall was one of these. This corn would then be ground and baked into bread for the Harvest Supper at the farm. Having this in mind, I mentioned the idea of making a loaf of bread to be sold the same day as its corn had been growing in the field. One Autumn day I did this. I arranged with a local farmer, Eric Wright from Gratwich, that he would let me know when he had cut a certain field of corn. This he did, and I collected the wheat, ground it and made it into bread – five cobs, in fact. These were put on display in the shop on the same day, with a short descriptive note about them. The bread would best be described as honey coloured. An Estonian fellow who had settled in this country begged and prayed of me to sell him one of these cobs. I gave him one, and next day he wanted to know if there would be more! Like others who had them, he enthused about the flavour, and told me that his brother had been a baker in Estonia. What did I think about it? Well – be in for a surprise – I dislike new bread and much prefer it a week old and burnt as black as coal, with plenty of butter on it!

CHAPTER TWENTY-TWO
Conclusion

Here at the Heath Bakery the range of goods embraces everything from bread rolls to wedding and birthday cakes and hot-plate goods are made twice a week – oatcakes and pikelets. Then there are such items as decorative bread for Harvest Festival services in many local Churches, and a lot of other seasonal goods which I have mentioned. All through my working life I was never completely satisfied with anything that I made! I was my own biggest critic and always tried to impove upon whatever I made, to try and attain perfection! Even the smallest imperfections had to face up to my own criticism, as I strove to reach the ideal. For example, a small cake or a bun would not have to be too small or it would betoken meanness and poor value for money. If too large it would be ugly and indelicate to eat in a clean and polite manner. If icing sugar was to be used for decoration it would not have to be too loud and garish, neither too pale or insipid. Neither over-baked nor under-baked, the article would have to be moist but firm enough to avoid creating a lot of crumbs when eaten. These were just a few of the criteria I looked for, but I insisted always on the purchase of good quality, wholesome ingredients, regardless of cost.

At the end of the day every cake or bun would appear on someone's tea table and its merits or otherwise would be appraised by someone else. This was the most important person in any business, the customer.

We are fortunate in having an infant's school just a stone's throw away from the bakehouse. Quite often, parties of children will pay us a visit, accompanied by their teacher. Our small bakery is nowadays more or less a working museum and the children love it, tramping up the old wooden stairs and other parts of the building; then watching the machines at work and hearing about dough being made with a living substance – yeast. They don't like the appearance of yeast and dislike its smell! Children always enjoy looking in the ovens and seeing goods being baked and watching us use the long wooden 'peels' for putting stuff in and out of the oven.

A peel in use by the author, drawing bread from the oven.

Then there are the very hot furnaces to be seen at the back of the ovens, all making towards a very enjoyable visit, more especially if each child is given a small cake or bun to take home with them! More important still, they each have a picture of work, production and reward impressed on their young and receptive minds. It is a scene which they will never forget, for all the rest of their time here on earth.

I suppose the infinite variety of work in a small bakehouse compensates in some way for the great amount of work which always needs to be done. My eldest son John now continues this business here at the Heath Bakery, fortunately with all the capability and tenacity required in these times of recession.

Perhaps as a young man I felt that there was no end to the constant and never changing pattern of sleep and work – work and sleep. Maybe hawking was a life of hard work, with little in the way of financial reward, but the greatest treasures in life were to be found there. Just like the Gospel – free and available to all who looked and could see them.

SOME BAKER'S UTENSILS

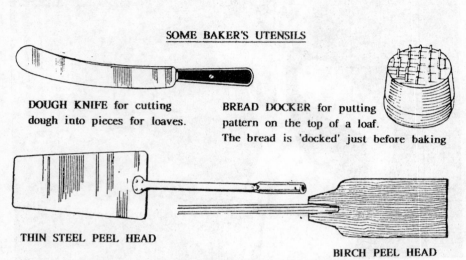

DOUGH KNIFE for cutting dough into pieces for loaves.

BREAD DOCKER for putting pattern on the top of a loaf. The bread is 'docked' just before baking

THIN STEEL PEEL HEAD

BIRCH PEEL HEAD

Peels were used for withdrawing bread from the oven.

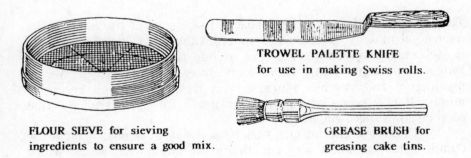

TROWEL PALETTE KNIFE for use in making Swiss rolls.

FLOUR SIEVE for sieving ingredients to ensure a good mix.

GREASE BRUSH for greasing cake tins.